RIVERS
of the
WORLD

The Mississippi

Titles in the Rivers of the World series include:

RIVERS
~ of the ~
WORLD

The Mississippi

Stephen Currie

LUCENT
BOOKS®

THOMSON
—— ✳ ——
GALE

San Diego • Detroit • New York • San Francisco • Cleveland • New Haven, Conn. • Waterville, Maine • London • Munich

On Cover: A fisherman stands on a sandbar in the Mississippi River
where it winds its way between the Minnesota and Wisconsin borders.

LIBRARY OF CONGRESS CATALOGING-IN-PUBLICATION DATA

Currie, Stephen, 1960–
　　The Mississippi / by Stephen Currie.
　　p. cm. — (Rivers of the world)
Summary: Discusses the importance of the Mississippi River, its role in the agricultural
and industrial development of the United States, floods and their impact, and various
threats to the river.
Includes bibliographical references and index.
　　ISBN 1-59018-061-5 (hardback: alk. paper)
　　1. Mississippi River—Juvenile literature. [†. Mississippi River.] I. Title. II. Series: Rivers of
the world (Lucent Books).
　　F351.C87 2003
　　977—dc21
　　　　　　　　　　　　　　　　　　　　　　　　　2002013088

Printed in the United States of America

Contents

• • • • • • • • • • • • • •

Foreword

......•••••••••

Human history and rivers are inextricably intertwined. Of all the geologic wonders of nature, none has played a more central and continuous role in the history of civilization than rivers. Fanning out across every major landmass except the Antarctic, all great rivers wove an arterial network that played a pivotal role in the inception of early civilizations and in the evolution of today's modern nation-states.

More than ten thousand years ago, when nomadic tribes first began to settle into small, stable communities, they discovered the benefits of cultivating crops and domesticating animals. These incipient civilizations developed a dependence on continuous flows of water to nourish and sustain their communities and food supplies. As small agrarian towns began to dot the Asian and African continents, the importance of rivers escalated as sources of community drinking water, as places for washing clothes, for sewage removal, for food, and as means of transportation. One by one, great riparian civilizations evolved whose collective fame is revered today, including ancient Mesopotamia, between the Tigris and Euphrates Rivers; Egypt, along the Nile; India, along the Ganges and Indus Rivers; and China, along the Yangtze. Later, for the same reasons, early civilizations in the Americas gravitated to the major rivers of the New World such as the Amazon, Mississippi, and Colorado.

For thousands of years, these rivers admirably fulfilled their role in nature's cycle of birth, death, and renewal. The waters also supported the rise of nations and their expanding populations. As hundreds and then thousands of cities sprang up along major rivers, today's modern nations emerged and discovered modern uses for the rivers. With more mouths to feed than ever before, great irrigation canals supplied by river water fanned out across the landscape, transforming parched land into mile upon mile of fertile cropland. Engineers developed the mathematics needed to throw great concrete dams across rivers to control occasional flooding and to store trillions of gallons of water to irrigate crops during the hot summer months. When the great age of electricity arrived, engineers added to the demands placed on rivers by using their cascading water to drive huge hydroelectric turbines to light and heat homes and skyscrapers in urban settings. Rivers also played a major role in the development of modern factories as sources of water for processing a variety of commercial goods and as a convenient place to discharge various types of refuse.

For a time, civilizations and rivers functioned in harmony. Such a benign relationship, however, was not destined to last. At the end of the twentieth century, scientists confirmed the opinions of environmentalists: The viability of all major rivers of the world was threatened. Urban populations could no longer drink the fetid water, masses of fish were dying from chemical toxins, and microorganisms critical to the food chain were disappearing along with the fish species at the top of the chain. The great hydroelectric dams had altered the natural flow of rivers, blocking migratory fish routes. As the twenty-first century unfolds, all who have contributed to spoiling the rivers are now in agreement that immediate steps must be taken to heal the rivers if their partnership with civilization is to continue.

Each volume in the Lucent Rivers of the World series tells the unique and fascinating story of a great river and its people. The significance of rivers to civilizations is emphasized to highlight both their historical role and the present situation. Each volume illustrates the idiosyncrasies of one great river in terms of its physical attributes, the plants and animals that depend on it, its role in ancient and modern cultures, how it served the needs of the people, the misuse of the river, and steps now being taken to remedy its problems.

Introduction

· · · · · · · · · · · · · · · · · · · ·

Two Rivers

By almost any standard, the Mississippi River is the most important river in the United States. With the possible exception of its tributary the Missouri, the Mississippi is the longest river on the North American continent. It winds more than twenty-three hundred miles from its source in Minnesota to southern Louisiana, where it spills into the Gulf of Mexico. The Mississippi carries a remarkable amount of water, too, dumping millions upon millions of gallons into the gulf every day. Its capacity and its length both place it among the great rivers of the world.

But perhaps the most important characteristic of the Mississippi is its location. It runs from north to south near the middle of the United States, cutting the nation very nearly in two and forming the borders of ten states. Moreover, the river lies at the center of an enormous drainage basin. The valley of the Mississippi encompasses all or part of thirty-one states, ranging from Montana and New Mexico to New York and Virginia. In all, the river drains more than 40 percent of U.S. territory outside Alaska and Hawaii, as well as a small section of Canada—perhaps one-eighth of the North American continent. The

Mississippi's basin dwarfs that of any other river world-wide but the Congo and the Amazon.

The Upper and Lower Rivers

The Mississippi frequently is viewed as two separate rivers. The Upper Mississippi consists of the northern half of the river, or the stretch lying between Lake Itasca, Minnesota, and Cairo, Illinois, where the Ohio River enters the main channel. The Lower Mississippi includes the rest of the river, flowing south from Cairo to the Gulf of Mexico. (For some geological purposes, the dividing line is considered to be north of Cairo, either at Cape Girardeau, Missouri, or just north of St. Louis at the confluence of the Mississippi and the Missouri Rivers.)

Mississippi River

The two sections of the river differ from each other in some important ways. The Upper Mississippi, for example, flows in places through hilly terrain. High rocky outcroppings known as bluffs line the riverbank along the Minnesota-Wisconsin border and extend, in places, into sections of Illinois and Missouri. The Lower Mississippi, in contrast, runs through much flatter country. Except for an occasional bluff, such as the one on which the town of Vicksburg, Mississippi, was constructed, the banks of the lower river are scarcely higher than the river itself.

The two sections also differ markedly in size. The Upper Mississippi is a large and wide river by any standard. In some places, the river widens enough to be considered a lake: For example, one twenty-mile stretch of the Mississippi between Wisconsin and Minnesota is nearly two miles across and is known as Lake Pepin. The Upper Mississippi is also wide enough to include at least five hundred islands large enough to have names. Some of these islands are several miles long.

Large as the Upper Mississippi is, though, it is dwarfed by the lower part of the river. The Lower Mississippi is not significantly wider than its northern counterpart—indeed, in many places it is not nearly as wide—but because it is deeper, it carries a great deal more water. At New Orleans, for instance, the lowest part of the riverbed is more than 170 feet below the surface of the water; in Minneapolis, in contrast, and indeed through much of the upper river, the depth rarely exceeds 10 to 12 feet. In fact, the last few hundred miles of the Lower Mississippi are so deep that the river bottom lies well below sea level.

Because of its great volume, the Lower Mississippi is, in general, much more powerful than the northern part of the river. The sheer mass of the water it carries gives it a force that the upper river cannot match. This strength gives the Lower Mississippi unique currents and causes it to behave in ways decidedly unlike most other rivers of the world. "[The river] moves south in layers and whorls," writes author John M. Barry, "like an uncoiling

The True River

The course of the Mississippi River is, in some sense, an accident of human history. There is no geological reason why the river is given one name from Minnesota to Louisiana, while other rivers that join it are considered its tributaries. The river is defined the way it is simply because of the pattern of early European exploration. The first French explorers entered the river from the north and traveled south, making arbitrary decisions as they passed each junction about which was the main stream and which a side current. Sometimes the answer was obvious; no one would mistake the Rock River in Illinois for the important channel, for example. Sometimes, though, the definitions were arbitrary indeed.

The St. Croix River, for example, could easily be considered more important than the Mississippi where the two join at Prescott, Wisconsin. At Prescott, the St. Croix flows more nearly north to south than does the Mississippi, which veers off to the west. If the Mississippi is considered a largely north-to-south river, it would make some sense to consider the St. Croix its true channel, making the northern stretches of the Mississippi simply a tributary. Similarly, because the Missouri is a great deal longer than the Mississippi at the point where the rivers meet, it might be reasonable to call the Mississippi the tributary.

Probably the strongest argument for primacy among the Mississippi's tributaries belongs to the Ohio. As Harlan Hubbard writes in *Shantyboat*, "If we had been the first explorers, the map we made would have indicated the Ohio as the main stream." That is partly because the Ohio seemed wider, Hubbard noted. More importantly, though, he added, "the river downstream carries out the contour of the Ohio, while the Mississippi seems to come in from the side." However, Hubbard did not get to draw the maps, and today the Mississippi takes in the Ohio rather than the other way around.

rope made up of a multitude of discrete fibers, each one following an independent and unpredictable path."[1]

Because of the varying terrain and the amount of water carried by the Lower Mississippi, the two halves of the river can strike an observer as almost wholly unrelated. The river changes as it moves below Cairo, looking and

A cargo ship makes its way down the Lower Mississippi, just north of New Orleans.

behaving differently than it did in its upper reaches. "It is no longer a sweet river," concludes Willard Price, who traveled the length of the river from Lake Itasca to Louisiana. "It is no longer pretty; it is majestic. It has lost its friendliness; now it is to be feared rather than loved."[2]

Contrasts notwithstanding, the Mississippi is indeed one river. Because of its central location, its navigability, and its size, it exerts a major influence over a huge portion of the United States. But of course the relationship works both ways. Just as the river affects the land and people who live in this enormous area, so too does human activity have an effect on the Mississippi. The relationship between the river and its people, through time, has often been an uneasy one.

1

• • • • • • • • • •

The Big Muddy

Although many small streams empty into Lake Itasca (pictured), this body of water is considered the source of the Mississippi.

By general consensus, the Mississippi is considered to begin at Lake Itasca in northwestern Minnesota. Such a specific designation of the Mississippi's source, however, is rather arbitrary. Lake Itasca itself is fed by a number of smaller streams, which in turn arise from a network of tiny ponds and underground springs nestled throughout the region. However, when explorer Henry Schoolcraft came into the area by boat in 1832, searching for the headwaters of the river, he concluded his journey at Lake Itasca; here the river, as it leaves the lake on its journey to the sea, is so small that people can easily jump across it. The small size of the stream, in Schoolcraft's eyes, qualified the lake as the river's origin.

From Lake Itasca, the Mississippi actually flows north for about sixty miles. Next, the river turns east toward Lake

What's in a Name?

The explorer Henry Schoolcraft gave Lake Itasca its name when he arrived in northwestern Minnesota in 1832. For many years, it was believed that the name was Native American in origin. Several linguists and anthropologists theorized that Itasca was a warrior, a divine spirit, or another important figure in the Ojibwa tradition. Others wondered if "Itasca" was a corruption of an Indian word used to describe natural features.

Then, early in the twentieth century, the mystery was solved. A scholar found a letter that Schoolcraft had written to an Illinois newspaper editor shortly after his journey. In the letter, Schoolcraft explained that the name "Itasca" had no connection whatsoever with Indian languages or peoples. Having found the headwaters of the Mississippi, Schoolcraft wrote, he named the lake after the Latin translation of the phrase "true head"— *veritas caput*. Then, because *veritas caput* sounded excessively long and ornate, Schoolcraft shortened it by removing the first syllable and the last. The result was "Itasca."

Thus, even the name of the lake reflects its status as the source of the Mississippi River.

Superior. After another hundred miles or so, however, the Mississippi begins to move south, which is the general direction it will take for the rest of its course. Growing steadily bigger as it takes in more and more streams from the surrounding countryside, the river slowly makes its way down the middle of the United States.

The mouth of the Mississippi lies in southeastern Louisiana, below the port of New Orleans. For most of its length, the Mississippi is made larger by the addition of other streams. Here at its mouth, however, the situation is reversed. As the channel approaches the Gulf of Mexico, the water spills off into several smaller channels, thereby forming a river delta. Just as there is no single source for the river, so there is no single mouth for it, only a series of channels, known as passes, that feed into the gulf itself.

Indeed, it can be difficult to distinguish where the river ends and where the Gulf of Mexico begins. In one sense, the lower stretches of the river are simply inlets of the sea. For example, there are noticeable tides in Baton Rouge, Louisiana, well over a hundred miles upriver of the Mississippi's mouth. The lands that make up the delta, in particular, are flat and so low that they barely rise above the surface of the water, and the channels are almost as salty as the sea itself. As a result, some argue that the river truly ends at a place called "Head of Passes," about eighty river miles downstream from New Orleans. Head of Passes is, as the name suggests, the point on the river from which the channels spring.

In another sense, though, the river flows well beyond Head of Passes—and even beyond the ends of the channels. According to this view, the river actually extends into the

This satellite photo shows the series of channels, or passes, by which the Mississippi empties into the Gulf of Mexico.

Gulf of Mexico. Far past the shore, the water that spills from the Mississippi can easily be distinguished from the waters of the gulf; the gulf water is blue, the Mississippi water is a darker brown. Looked at in that way, the river can be thought to continue even after it moves into the ocean.

Curves and Meanders

Between its start and finish, the river's course is somewhat atypical of the great rivers of the world. Unlike, for example, the Nile, the Hudson, and many other great rivers, the Mississippi does not usually flow in a straight path. Instead, it curves and meanders throughout much of its route.

This meandering is evident along the Upper Mississippi, which swings in great east-west arcs throughout most of its journey south. Between Minneapolis and LaCrosse, Wisconsin, for example, the river travels a more easterly than southerly course. A few hundred miles downstream, the Mississippi veers almost due west again as the river flows away from Davenport, Iowa. Farther south, near St. Louis, the river again flows northward for a few miles; it does so once more a short distance upriver from Cairo, Illinois.

But the curves particularly distinguish the lower part of the river. From Cairo to the Gulf of Mexico is a straight-line distance of about six hundred miles. The Mississippi, however, takes almost twice as many miles to connect the two points. The lower half of the river is full of long and winding loops that wander erratically to one side and then to the other. Often the channel very nearly doubles back on itself, taking five or six miles to travel a distance that might be as little as five or six hundred yards in a straight line over the land.

The meandering is partly determined by the surrounding countryside. Even the upper stretches of the river run through relatively flat terrain—the bluffs of Wisconsin, after all, can hardly be characterized as mountains.

Furthermore, the Mississippi has an extremely gentle slope. Between Minneapolis and New Orleans, the river descends only about eight hundred feet—just a few inches for every mile of channel. Thus, along much of the river's length, no natural features prevent it from going wherever it is inclined to go. As a result, the Mississippi is perpetually changing course. As writer John McPhee describes the process along the lower part of the river, the river "has jumped here and there within an arc about two hundred miles wide, like a pianist playing with one hand."[3]

Loops, Oxbows, and Cutoffs

Often, the changes in the river's course are gradual and subtle. That is especially evident in the creation of the broad loops and the small islands common to the river. Over a period of several decades, for example, the steady pressure of the current flowing through a bend can carve out a longer and wider curve; or the constant accumulation of mud in one straight section may slowly build a tiny sandbar into an island. These changes would be impossible to notice from day to day, and would be difficult to recognize even from one year to the next.

The Mississippi also has a tendency to move gradually sideways. Over time, the current may erode one bank of the river more than the opposite side. As the water moves in the new direction, the other bank begins to dry up. The process is slow, but can have a remarkable effect over time. "Nearly the whole of that one thousand three hundred miles of old Mississippi River which [explorer Robert] La Salle floated down in his canoes, two hundred years ago, is good solid dry ground now," wrote Mark Twain in 1883. "The river lies to the right of it, in places, and to the left of it in other places."[4]

But the Mississippi's course can also change quickly and dramatically. In its constantly shifting route to the sea, the river often cuts through the narrow pieces of land that separate the loops from one another. These changes have sudden and significant effects on the river as a whole. Granted a new and faster passage south through these new channels—usually called cutoffs—the water abandons the old loop and surges instead down the newly created path. Before long, the old loop is separated completely from the rest of the river. For a time, the former channel remains as an oxbow, or crescent-shaped lake. Eventually, though, deprived of a source of additional water, the oxbow simply dries up.

Through history, the river has created dozens upon dozens of new cutoffs. The consequences for the people

In this aerial photograph, crescent-shaped lakes known as oxbows are visible to the left of the present course of the Mississippi.

New Madrid and Reelfoot Lake

Sometimes the changes in the Mississippi's course can be even more dramatic than the sudden opening of a new cutoff. In 1811 and 1812, for instance, a series of four earthquakes rocked the territory around the town of New Madrid, in the southeastern corner of Missouri. The aftershocks of the quakes were felt for hundreds of miles, and walls shook and chimneys tumbled in cities as distant from the site as St. Louis and Cincinnati. The immediate area of the tremor was thinly settled, so there were few casualties; but by the fourth and last of the earthquakes, all the buildings in and around New Madrid had been thoroughly destroyed.

The earthquakes played havoc with the surrounding countryside, too. The sudden split in the subterranean rocks raised some sections of the riverbed while lowering other parts of the terrain. As Hodding Carter puts it in *Lower Mississippi*, "High bluffs disappeared, riverbanks were swallowed, entire islands caved out of sight into the river." The new terrain forced the river into a brand-new path, in some places many miles from the old one.

The earthquakes also resulted in the creation of Reelfoot Lake in Tennessee. Eighteen miles long, two miles wide, and extremely shallow, it is the remnant of an earlier course taken by the river. Dammed at both ends by the earthquake, the water was trapped while the river directed its flow elsewhere. Reelfoot Lake still exists, a monument to the powerful forces of nature.

who live on the river's banks have been dramatic. The town of Kaskaskia, Illinois, for instance, began its existence east of the Mississippi. But after the town was built, the river cut itself a new route several miles to the east. Today, Kaskaskia sits on the west bank of the river, connected by land to neighboring Missouri but on the opposite side of the water from the rest of Illinois. Other towns have had to be moved to avoid being washed away by these sorts of shifts in the river. The nearby town of New Madrid, Missouri, for instance, has been moved four times for this reason. Its first sites are now either underwater, or across the river in what is now Kentucky.

Tributaries

Another of the Mississippi's defining characteristics is the number of its tributaries. Because it drains most of the United States between the Rocky Mountains to the west and the Appalachians to the east, the Mississippi incorporates many other rivers into its channel along its path. These rivers increase the volume, width, and power of the river as it makes its way to the Gulf of Mexico.

The most important of these tributaries have a measurable effect on the course and the strength of the Mississippi. This list includes the Missouri, the Ohio, the Arkansas, and several other well-known rivers, some of which are virtually as large as the Mississippi itself. The Ohio, for instance, is nearly the same width as the Mississippi where the two rivers join near Cairo, Illinois. And the Missouri River travels about twenty-three hundred miles to its junction with Mississippi north of St. Louis—more or less the length of the entire Mississippi.

The Mississippi has countless smaller tributaries as well. The major tributaries have minor tributaries of their own. The Tennessee, for instance, flows into the Ohio and from there into the Mississippi; so do the Cumberland, the Wabash, and the Monongahela, among others. The Platte River, similarly, runs into the Missouri, and the Canadian River flows into the Arkansas. While these rivers do not flow directly into the Mississippi, they still count as tributaries, since the water they carry affects the flow of the Mississippi.

And some of the river's tributaries are small indeed. Most of the Mississippi basin receives heavy rainfall, and that precipitation supports the flow of hundreds of permanent creeks and streams, as well as a few that flow only in the spring and early summer. Though these channels typically carry little water, they eventually spill into the river. Counting these streams lifts the census of Mississippi tributaries into the hundred thousand range.

Each major tributary has an effect on the main body of the Mississippi. In some cases, the main result is simply to

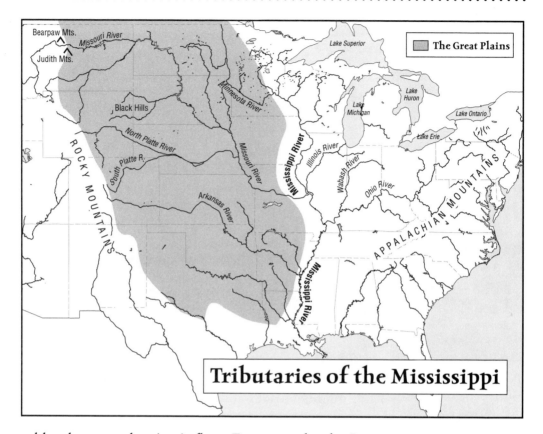

Tributaries of the Mississippi

add volume to the river's flow. For example, the Lower Mississippi's extra depth is almost entirely due to the water poured into it by rivers farther upstream. But the tributaries create other changes in the river, too. A few of the rivers that flow into the Mississippi have different depths, chemical compositions, or temperatures than the Mississippi itself. As the waters are joined, these factors affect the Mississippi as it flows south, changing its character significantly.

The Minnesota River, for example, has a noticeably different color from the Mississippi. Viewed from a distance where the rivers meet near Minneapolis, the Mississippi is dark blue, while the Minnesota is a grayish green because it carries much more sediment, or silt, than the Mississippi. The silt from the Minnesota, combined with the sediment from many other tributaries farther downstream, makes

The waters of the Minnesota River (left) converge with the Mississippi near Minneapolis.

the Mississippi—relatively clear at its headwaters—one of the muddiest rivers on Earth by the time it reaches the gulf.

Sediment

The Mississippi is indeed full of mud. Many of the river's nicknames, in fact, make reference to the enormous amount of sediment the Mississippi carries. The river is frequently known today as the Big Muddy, for instance, but this is only one of several such nicknames: One early observer referred to the river, only half jokingly, as "the Great Sewer."[5]

One reason so much sediment ends up in the river is that the land through which the river runs is so flat. During periods of heavy rain, water streams across the land and into nearby rivers and lakes. In hilly territory, the water moves quickly down the slopes, taking very little of the surrounding soil with it. In flatter land, however, the slow-flowing rainwater has more time to loosen and pick up the topsoil and carry it along. Throughout the Midwest and into the South, the river is constantly picking up particles of earth. The individual grains are too small to see clearly, but in large numbers they appear as a muddy cloud, suspended in the current and traveling quickly downstream.

The amount of sediment is remarkable. When the water levels are high and its sediment load is at its peak, the river disgorges several million tons of earth each day into the Gulf of Mexico. Even when sediment levels are relatively low, the river still deposits at least half a million tons of dirt each day into the sea. And what washes out the southern end of the river is only part of the river's load. Much, perhaps most, of the silt never makes it to the Gulf of Mexico; instead, the river dumps it onto its banks along its route.

The sediment has a number of effects on the river. Most obviously, the mud swirling through the stream gives the Mississippi a distinctive brownish tinge, especially as the river creeps south. The sediment also plays an important role in the constant rerouting of the river. If enough dirt is deposited in a certain location, for example, then the main channel through that stretch is narrowed; flowing faster as a result, the current may gather enough force to create a cutoff downstream. In other cases, the piled-up dirt creates a barrier to the water's flow, forcing the river to make a loop or another detour in its journey toward the gulf.

Likewise, sediment buildup along the bottom of the river can create sandbars and islands, which also affect the Mississippi's path. When the river is obstructed by an island, the channel must divide in two. One of those new channels is usually deeper, smoother, and more free-flowing. Over time, the water tends more and more to move in that direction, causing the other channel to gradually become shallower. The sediment washed from upstream, in turn, piles up in the slower-moving, shallower channel. Eventually, the mud closes off the channel altogether, joining the island to the riverbank.

Sediment carried downstream by the Mississippi has built up to create this series of islands in southern Louisiana.

Such changes can occur slowly, but they can also take place with surprising speed. Even large and seemingly permanent landforms are not exempt from the river's power. "A big island that used to be away out in mid-river," reported Mark Twain about thirty years after his days as a river pilot came to an end, "has retired to the Missouri shore, and boats do not go near it any more."[6] This island was only one of many that had been created, washed away, or absorbed into the mainland since he had last visited the river.

The mud does not come to rest evenly along the course of the river. Earth is more likely to be deposited along slow sections of the Mississippi, for example, than in places where the current moves along swiftly. Similarly, more mud piles up along the curves of the river than along the Mississippi's straighter stretches. But even sections of the river in which little sediment is deposited are affected by the presence of the mud elsewhere. The narrowing, deepening, or rerouting of one stretch of the river necessarily changes the way the water flows downstream from that point.

Sediment and the Lower Mississippi Valley

Through history, the amount of sediment in the river has played important roles. In geological terms, the Lower Mississippi is a very young river, far newer than the river's upper stretches or many other rivers around the world. Long after the Upper Mississippi was established, the lower part of the river quite literally did not exist. Thousands of years ago, the Mississippi ended near where the Ohio meets it today. To the south of that point was open ocean.

Over time, though, that changed. Sea levels gradually lowered, pushing the gulf slowly to the south and exposing land beneath the waters. However, the underlying land was so flat and sloped so gently to the sea that the water did not drain easily from it. Absent any other influences, all the area south of where Cairo, Illinois, is now located would have become an estuary, or a long tidal wetland. Like the swamps of southern Louisiana today, the land would have been covered for most of the year by a layer of water several inches to several feet deep, with only occasional areas of high ground remaining dry throughout the year.

The Upper Mississippi, however, changed that. The sediment it washed into the retreating gulf came to rest along the edges of the river's mouth. As more and more mud flowed down the river, the excess sediment built into piles that were higher and wider; they also stretched farther and farther south. The result was a river that grew ever longer, eventually snaking its way another six hundred straight-line miles to the current boundaries of the gulf. In other words, the river was laying down land where none had existed before. Over the years, the river

The Dis-Tributary

Most rivers are fed by tributaries as they run downstream, just as the Mississippi is. Less common is the permanent splitting of the channel. Rivers typically do not break into parts until they are near their end, but the land through which the Lower Mississippi flows is so flat that it does exactly that several times throughout its route.

Of these "dis-tributaries," the most important is the Atchafalaya River, which springs from the Mississippi in northeastern Lousiana and makes its own way to the Gulf of Mexico many miles to the parent river's west. The Atchafalaya presents an interesting and difficult problem for river engineers. The smaller river moves more quickly down a steeper slope, and is in some ways the more natural channel for the river to take. Left to its own devices, the Mississippi would quickly change its course, with the bulk of the water heading down the Atchafalaya in preference to its usual path.

Such a change, however, could be potentially disastrous. The diversion of water to the Atchafalaya would leave New Orleans and Baton Rouge high and dry, seriously damaging the economy of much of southeastern Louisiana. The loss of water would affect wildlife in the area, too. At the same time, if the extra water came rushing down the Atchafalaya, communities along that river would be flooded, and the swamps and marshes in the region would be devastated by the sudden influx of fresh water.

A strong wall placed at one side of the channel currently keeps the water from following its more natural course. However, some observers doubt that the river can be permanently stopped from rushing down the Atchafalaya at the end of its run. The Mississippi, in this view, is simply too powerful to be contained.

The Atchafalaya River in northeastern Louisiana is the most significant stream arising from the Mississippi.

has deposited about thirteen hundred cubic miles of sediment into the region surrounding the Lower Mississippi. The states of the lower river, thus, owe their existence to the mud carried down the river from upstream.

The laying of sediment continues today. Even during recorded history, the river has visibly extended itself into the Gulf of Mexico. The Mississippi routinely forms sandbars and other obstructions at its mouth, thus pushing its channels farther and farther into the sea. The southeastern tip of Louisiana is a clear demonstration of the process. It juts into the gulf, a narrow projection of land surrounding the river, its banks the result of the thousands of tons of sediment washing downstream. Since the time of the earliest settlers, the land has extended a few extra miles into the gulf, and each year, if imperceptibly, it moves a little farther. "The process is still going on," remarked writer Hodding Carter in 1942. "It always will."[7]

2

....

The River as Highway

Since the earliest times, the Mississippi River has been used to move people and goods quickly and efficiently. Indeed, the Mississippi is one of the world's most easily navigable rivers. Large oceangoing vessels today can travel up the river as far as Baton Rouge, well over a hundred miles from the Mississippi's mouth. Barges loaded with cargo can journey as far as Minneapolis—a distance of about two thousand river miles from the Gulf of Mexico. Smaller boats and pleasure craft can travel the river nearly to its source at Lake Itasca. And many of the Mississippi's important tributaries—the Arkansas, the Ohio, the Illinois, and the Missouri, in particular—are easily traveled, too.

The Mississippi's navigability results largely from its topography. The generally flat terrain through which the river travels makes for a relatively smooth current. And although the current can travel with great speed, the Mississippi's gentle rate of descent makes it possible to propel a boat upstream, or against the natural flow of the river, largely unimpeded by rapids or waterfalls. St. Anthony's Falls in Minneapolis, two thousand miles above the river's mouth, is the southernmost waterfall on the river.

Navigational Issues

This is not to say that navigating the Mississippi is easy. Generations of travelers have noted that the river can be deceptive and dangerous. The loops and bends typical of the lower river can be difficult to negotiate, for example. The currents in such areas can easily change speeds and catch an unwary boater by surprise, upsetting the craft or smashing it against the riverbank. Similarly, the Mississippi often forms whirlpools, or eddies, which can wreak havoc with watercraft that get caught in them. One observer described an eddy "running upstream at seven miles an hour and extending across half the river, whirling and foaming."[8] Such forces make navigation on the river a complicated business.

The river's uneven depth has made its navigation famously tricky. The Mississippi forms sandbars in unexpected places, even directly in the middle of an otherwise free-flowing channel, making the river too shallow in some places for all but a few types of boats. Other shallow spots along the river are treacherous in other ways: They harbor tree limbs and other obstacles that can damage or destroy a vessel that runs into them. Jonathan Raban, who took a motorboat down much of the river in 1980, ran into one such area on the Wisconsin-Minnesota border. "As far as one could see," he wrote, "rotten tree trunks stood up, some just below, some a few inches above the water. . . . The river slurped around their blackened roots."[9]

Yet despite the significant navigational problems it presents, the river remains a valuable way of transporting goods and people. Today, shipping continues to be of great importance to Mississippi River towns and cities. Indeed, travel along the river has helped make the United States what it is today.

The Mississippians

The relative ease of traveling on the river has encouraged exploration, settlement, and economic growth along its banks since prehistoric times. Between 800 and 1500, the banks of the Mississippi River were inhabited largely by a people known today as Mississippians. The Mississippian culture extended over a wide geographic area that included much of the Ohio River Valley as well as most of the Lower and parts of the Upper Mississippi. Mississippians typically lived in permanent settlements, some quite large, such as Cahokia on the eastern side of the Mississippi near modern-day St. Louis. The Mississippians had a complex society and an economy based largely on trade.

These ancient mounds near St. Louis are part of Cahokia, the remains of a settlment inhabited by a people known today as Mississippians.

The Mississippians were indeed great traders, and the rivers, particularly the Mississippi, played an important role in their activities. River travel was generally easier than carrying goods overland through the thick forests

that flanked the river. The Mississippians had no horses or other pack animals to carry loads or to pull wagons and carts. But they did know how to make and handle watercraft. The residents of Cahokia, for example, hollowed out logs to form dugout canoes and paddled up and down the river, trading with people they encountered along the way.

This ancient amulet created by a Mississippian artisan depicts a winged shaman holding a human head (left).

Exactly how far any individual trader traveled is anybody's guess. It is possible that a trip could have lasted for weeks and covered hundreds of miles. Probably, though, traders mastered a relatively small and familiar territory along the Mississippi. Trade goods were thus passed from one trader to the next, slowly making their way up the river one village at a time.

However the procedure actually worked, without the river and the trade it permitted, Mississippian peoples clearly could never have developed a society as complex as theirs. Cahokia's waterfront, suggests one writer, "must have been a bustling place where large dugout canoes laden with raw materials from afar docked and then shipped out with...desired trade items."[10] The thriving commercial networks brought goods and information to the Mississippians that they would not otherwise have had.

Later Native Americans

The Mississippian culture probably reached its peak between about 1000 and 1300 and, for reasons that are unclear, declined rather swiftly after that. The native cultures that took their place, however, also used the river for travel, particularly those tribes, such as the Chickasaw and the Yaddo, that lived along the Lower Mississippi. The low-lying ground along the southern stretches of the river was prone to flooding. Swamps covered much of the region as well. In some areas of the Lower Mississippi, overland travel was practically impossible. Boats were therefore a necessity for those who ventured more than a few hundred yards from their homes.

Like the Mississippians who came before them, the later Indians of the lower river preferred dugout canoes to any other kind of boat. These boats were often large and elaborate: The most complex, writes historian Norbury L. Wayman, "were over thirty feet long, with a beam of four feet or more, with a mast and sail amidships."[11] The Choctaw, in particular, were known for the sturdiness and maneuverability of their dugouts. Again like the Mississippians, the Choctaw and the other groups of the Lower Mississippi used the dugouts for trading purposes; they also used their canoes to help them in hunting and fishing.

The Indians of the Upper Mississippi made use of the river, too, but as a means of travel it was less important to them, since the surrounding terrain was much easier to cross than it was in the south. Trees and vines did not grow as densely in the forests of the north, and there were fewer swamps and other barriers to movement on foot. By the eighteenth century, too, a number of Native American peoples had started to use horses, introduced to the New World by Spanish explorers; the horses made land travel that much simpler, especially in the relatively open terrain of upper North America.

Another reason for the river's lesser importance to the northern Indians involved climate. During the winter the northern stretches of the river froze solid, making navigation impossible for long periods. Nor, for that matter, was a boat as useful away from the river's main channel in the north as it was in the south. The land near the Upper Mississippi was not nearly as wet as land near the lower river, and the Upper Mississippi had fewer oxbows and backwaters.

The peoples of the Upper Mississippi who traveled on the river usually did not use the dugout canoes popular among the Choctaw and the Yaddo, although the Illinois tribe did make dugouts from butternut trees. More often, the Native Americans of the north made canoes from birchbark. These craft usually were built for just one or two people. A few, though, designed for hunting parties, bands of warriors, or groups of traders, could accommodate four, six, or even ten paddlers at a time.

Early Adventurers from Europe

Unlike the Indians, the first Europeans to see the Mississippi saw little value in the river as a means of travel. In 1519, soon after Columbus arrived in the New World, a Spaniard named Alonzo Alvarez de Pineda sailed into the mouth of the Mississippi, becoming the first European to travel on the river. Pineda probably did not go more than a few miles upriver, however, and the reports of his journey he brought back to Spanish leaders did not encourage other adventurers to go farther.

Not until 1542 did another European even lay eyes on the Mississippi. That was Pineda's fellow Spaniard Hernando de Soto, who stumbled upon the river near the site of modern-day Memphis while making an overland expedition in search of gold. But de Soto was not much impressed by the river. By the time he and his followers reached the river, they were tired, sick, and discouraged by an unsuccessful expedition that had already lasted several years. To them, the river was nothing more than an obstacle to be overcome in order to move farther west.

One of de Soto's men, however, did include a useful piece of information in his account of the journey. The explorers, he wrote, "found that there was an abundance of timber near [the river] from which piraguas [a kind of dugout boat] could be constructed."[12] De Soto's purpose in crafting the boats was simply to cross the river so as to

Hernando de Soto, shown in this painting, reached the banks of the Mississippi in 1542.

continue his search for gold to the west. But later explorers would find the boats even more useful in traveling up and down the river.

A European Highway

Serious exploration of the Mississippi River did not begin, though, until well over a century after de Soto's visit. The Spanish, obsessed with the quest for gold, mounted large expeditions weighed down with equipment that made river travel impractical. The French, on the other hand, were more interested in spreading Christianity to the Indians than in acquiring material wealth. Thus, they sent out smaller, lightly equipped expeditions, and these were better able to use the rivers as highways.

The first of these expeditions was led by a soldier, Louis Jolliet, and a Roman Catholic priest, Father Jacques Marquette. The two left Lake Michigan in the spring of 1673, portaged their canoes to the Wisconsin River, and

Hernando de Soto's Adventure

One member of Hernando de Soto's expedition wrote an account of his journey. His actual name is unknown; he is believed to be Portuguese in origin and is usually referred to simply as the Gentleman of Elvas. Whatever his identity, he wrote a brief description of the Mississippi upon encountering it for the first time, as quoted in Hodding Carter's Lower Mississippi:

[De Soto] went to see the river and found there was an abundance of timber near it from which piraguas [boats] could be constructed, and an excellently situated land for establishing the camp. [The river] was nearly half a league [that is, a mile and a half] wide, and if a man stood still on the other side one could not tell whether he were a man or something else. It was of a great depth, and of very strong current. Its waters were always turgid and continually many trees and wood came down it, borne along by the force of the current. . . . It had [an] abundance of fish of various kinds and most of them [were] different from those of the fresh waters of Spain.

Exactly where de Soto and his men ran into the Mississippi is unclear. Certainly the description could apply to most of the lower part of the river. The most likely candidates lie in what is now northern Mississippi, somewhere between present-day Tunica County and the city of Memphis, Tennessee. De Soto crossed the river and spent most of the next year traveling in the Southwest before returning to the Mississippi. By this time, however, he was very sick indeed. He died shortly afterwards, somewhere along the banks of the river which he had seen only as an obstruction.

Native American guides accompany French explorer Louis Jolliet and Father Jacques Marquette on their 1673 expedition.

followed the Wisconsin west to the Mississippi. Next they paddled several hundred miles downriver to just below the mouth of the Arkansas, before returning by way of the Illinois River.

Word of the experiences of Marquette and Jolliet set off a flurry of exploration. In 1682, René-Robert La Salle led a journey down the Mississippi from the mouth of the Illinois all the way to the Gulf of Mexico. La Salle claimed the entire river for France, then headed back north. In the meantime, La Salle's partner, Louis Hennepin, headed north to explore the Upper Mississippi. Although he was captured and briefly held at one point by members of the Dakota tribe, Hennepin managed to reach the site of present-day Minneapolis. After years of ignoring the river, European explorers had traversed all but its northernmost stretches—and had done so in less than a decade.

The availability of easily navigable waterways like the Mississippi would have an important effect on the development of what one day would be the United States. Like the Native Americans before them, the French recognized that river travel was far simpler than overland travel. Moreover, nearly all the rivers affording access to the lands between the Rockies and the Appalachians drained into the Mississippi. Thus, the Mississippi allowed travelers a relatively straightforward path into the interior of the continent. Without the river, exploration and settlement of North America by Europeans would have been much slower and more difficult.

The river was of great strategic importance as well. The French recognized that just as goods could flow up and down the river, as they had done in Mississippian times, so too could soldiers and settlers. Whoever controlled the river could control colonization and trade within the continent's interior.

Traders, Soldiers, and Settlers

Over the next century, the French took the lead among Europeans in laying claim to much of the Mississippi basin. Trappers and fur traders came first, traveling up the river in search of pelts from beaver, mink, otter, and other native mammals. For these trappers, many but not all of them French, the river was the most convenient means of getting to places where the animals could be found.

The river was also the best way for the traders to get their goods to market. Outposts devoted to buying and shipping furs soon sprang up along the banks of the Mississippi. Many river towns, such as New Madrid, Missouri, were originally centers of the fur trade. Indeed, early European settlement in the central part of North America was concentrated along the river.

Other early European settlements along the river had military purposes. Fort Chartres, near Kaskaskia, Illinois, was one of many French garrisons on the banks of the river. Spain likewise set up several forts along the lower part of the Mississippi. Later on, England set up forts along the river, after the peace treaty that ended the

Flatboats and Keelboats

Flatboats and keelboats were the most common method of transportation along the Mississippi River during the first years of the 1800s. Neither made travel easy. Flatboats, similar in some ways to modern barges, were up to sixty feet long and built low. At the front and sides of the boats, the deck was elevated only about three feet above the water's surface. Because they were used for transporting passengers as well as cargo, the flatboats' decks supported much higher structures: Their owners constructed cabins and other housing on board, which unfortunately tended to destabilize the craft.

Flatboats were hard to maneuver, too. Long oars stuck out to the side and in the front of the vessel. Captains could approximate a course by shifting the angle of the oars. Still, steering was a tricky business, and few flatboat pilots could actually get their boats to go where they wished.

The keelboats were somewhat more effective. Longer, wider, and sleeker than the flatboat, the keelboat was generally better balanced as well. It was also possible to maneuver them upstream, although the work was backbreakingly difficult. As Norbury Wayman describes the process in *Life on the River:*

"Running along each side [of the keelboat] was a narrow gangway. This was used for a walkway for a crew of four or five men on each side, who would thrust poles into the river bottom and, on command, walk toward the stern while leaning on the poles, thereby propelling the boat forward in shallow water." Where the water was deeper, the men rowed or set up a sail if the current and wind permitted. Where this was not possible, the crewmen got out and dragged the boat along the shore by means of a towrope, also known as a cordelle. "Keelboat men," observes Wayman, "were a lusty lot, exceptionally muscular from poling and rowing, and threw their weight around. They were . . . heavy drinkers and great fighters . . . constantly looking for a contest."

Flatboats such as the one shown in this 1898 photo were once a common mode of travel on the Mississippi.

French and Indian War in 1763 granted England virtually all the territory east of the river.

Full-scale settlement of the Mississippi region, however, did not begin until the early nineteenth century, by pioneers of an entirely new nation: the United States of America. Eager to claim land away from the settled Atlantic seaboard, these newly independent Americans headed west, attracted by the fertile lands and tall forests of the Mississippi Valley. They soon found that the going was easiest by river. Prospective settlers constructed boats out of any available materials and floated down the Ohio River and its tributaries. Some stopped along the way, in Kentucky or Indiana, but others continued to drift until they reached the Mississippi. From there, they branched out again. Many followed the current south; others headed north.

Like the trappers and traders before them, these pioneers settled close to the rivers. By 1820, hundreds of small farms and dozens of villages were to be found within a few miles of the Mississippi's banks. Just ten or twenty miles away from the river was wilderness. This settlement pattern made sense. The settlers had come down the rivers, and they saw no point in dragging their belongings overland when there was land to be had just by putting ashore. In a very real sense, the map of the rivers of the Mississippi Valley was a map of the settlement of the interior of the United States.

Trade and Politics

The nineteenth century saw a boom in the populations and prospects of many river cities. By the time of the Civil War, New Orleans was the largest city in the South, and despite a late start St. Louis had become one of the largest cities of the North. Other, newer, cities grew too. Memphis became a large and important community soon after its founding in the 1820s. Even the city of St. Paul, far up the river in east central Minnesota, had become a populous territorial and state capital by the 1850s.

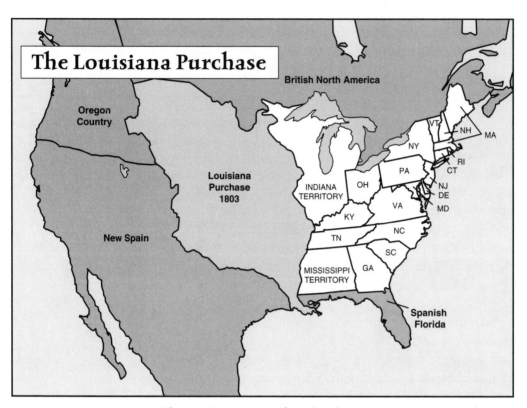

The Louisiana Purchase

British North America

Oregon Country

Louisiana Purchase 1803

New Spain

INDIANA TERRITORY

OH

PA

NY

VT

NH

MA

RI

CT

NJ

DE

MD

VA

KY

TN

NC

SC

GA

MISSISSIPPI TERRITORY

Spanish Florida

The main reason for the boom was river trade. As they had during the fur traders' heyday, boats plied the Mississippi from one port to the next. By the nineteenth century, the fur trade had moved north and west, so these boats mostly carried grain, lumber, and livestock. Well before the Civil War, a network of trade had sprung up, one a good deal more complex than that established by the Mississippians.

The growth of this trading network was possible for two important reasons. The first was political. In 1803, the United States purchased the Louisiana Territory from France. This territory encompassed most of the western half of the Mississippi basin and all of the river's mouth. Since most territory to the east of the river already belonged to the United States, the purchase thus gave Americans complete control over the river and most of its tributaries.

As France had recognized years earlier, whoever controlled the river could control settlement and commerce along its banks as well. Before the Louisiana Purchase, Americans had been intrigued by the potential of river commerce, but because the entire river did not belong to them, they had been reluctant to invest much time, money, and energy into developing it. There was always the chance that Americans would find the river—especially its mouth—closed to them entirely. When the United States gained full control of the channel, the possibility of closure was eliminated, and trade received an important boost.

The Steamboat Era

The other reason for the increased trade was the development of new and improved technology. In the early days of Mississippi travel, explorers and settlers had either propelled their crafts with muscle power or allowed the current to carry them along. Most of these watercraft were simple rafts, lashed together with rope and steered with a single long paddle at the stern. But even the more sophisticated designs suffered from an important problem: The river's current made it hard to move upstream.

Thus, river travel was a slow and arduous business. A vessel could float or be rowed south along the Mississippi, but coming north again was another matter entirely. Many river traders sold or abandoned their boats once they reached New Orleans. They would then return to the northern stretches of the river by heading out overland, following a route that Wayman describes as "frequented by murderous highwaymen."[13] Alternatively, the rivermen pushed, poled, and dragged their boats back up the river, but the return journey took too long and used up too much energy to make the effort worthwhile.

This situation changed with Robert Fulton's development of the first practical steamboat in 1807. The steamboat made it possible to travel almost as easily upstream as downstream. By the 1830s, steamboats made the cities of the Mississippi among the most thriving commercial centers anywhere in the country. In 1839, the level of trade in New Orleans matched that of New York City. St. Louis's port handled fifteen thousand pounds of goods in 1822, before the steamboat was in widespread use; by 1842, it handled half a million. The steamboat made river commerce practical and profitable.

Steamboats also carried people. Laborers, immigrants, and families looking to leave the settled East crowded onto steamers and headed up the river. "The rapid growth and settlement of the Upper Midwest was because of the paddlewheel steamer,"[14] one writer concludes. Settlement no doubt would have continued had the steamboat never appeared, but the process was hastened by this new and improved form of transportation.

However, steamboat travel carried risk. Steamboat captains and companies were eager to fit on as many passengers or goods as possible, often without regard to the boat's actual carrying capacity. Sometimes overloaded

Steamboats such as these boosted commerce along the Mississippi by enabling passengers and cargo to travel upstream as easily as downstream.

Showboat!

One of the most colorful and intriguing methods of travel on the Mississippi was the showboat. Showboats were floating theaters that moved up and down the waters of the river during much of the nineteenth century, stopping in little towns as they traveled. They were particularly common in the southern part of the river, although some showboats made stops along the Upper Mississippi as well. Most of these boats were quite small, but a few grew to surprising proportions: One showboat owned and run by Callie and Augustus French seated 950.

Showboat companies put on a variety of performances for paying customers. Callie French, for instance, not only acted and sang, but played the calliope and walked the tightrope as well. However, showboats were best known for presenting melodrama: poorly written plays with heavy-handed moral lessons, easily identifiable heroes and villains, and endings in which good invariably triumphed. The acting was often atrocious.

Nevertheless, audiences flocked to see the shows. Great excitement was generated by the presence of a showboat in a community: In many towns, commerce essentially ground to a halt until the actors headed elsewhere. In an era before television, movies, and widespread road travel, the showboats provided entertainment for the residents of small river towns. Most cared little about the quality of the product: Bad acting and poor scripts could be overlooked in the enthusiasm of seeing a real show.

vessels literally sank under the excess weight. Navigation in the shallow fast-moving current was dangerous, too. The *Tennessee*, for instance, was destroyed by an underwater snag in 1823, and sixty passengers drowned as a result. And the massive boilers of the early-nineteenth-century steamboats had an unfortunate tendency to explode. In 1852 the *Glencoe* blew up near St. Louis; the death toll from the blast included virtually all aboard along with six people aboard a nearby vessel.

For Native Americans, the consequences of the steamboats' arrival were even worse. Settlers, many arriving by boat, took the lands Native Americans had occupied for generations. When the Indians objected, troops forcibly removed them, killing many in the process. When the Sac Indians of Wisconsin protested the government's land policies in 1832, for instance, the army outfitted a steamboat with weapons and sent it to the region. "She fired with cannon into the massed crowd of Indian men, women, and children," wrote steamboat historians Herbert and Edward Quick, "and followed with musketry." Most of the Indians in the group were killed, although there was no evidence that the Sac had planned any sort of attack. According to the Quicks, "Seldom have troops and steamboats been used in ways less creditable."[15]

Barges

Steamboating gradually became less important as the nineteenth century wore on. The Civil War seriously damaged the shipping industry; through much of the war control of the river was divided between North and South, and all but local trade became difficult or impossible. After the war, the steamboats faced a new and more permanent threat: the railroads. Trains soon proved faster and more efficient at carrying passengers and most freight. Moreover, rails could be laid virtually anywhere, allowing trains to serve settlements located far from navigable rivers. By the late 1800s, railroads connected most large cities along the Mississippi, and the great days of steamboating were over.

River shipping, however, did not die. Today, commodities such as grain, coal, and oil are shipped on massive barges with far greater capacity than the trains. Powerful tugboats propel several barges at a time from one river terminal to another. Perhaps 100 million tons of these goods are carried each year by barge along the Mississippi.

To accommodate this river traffic, the U.S. Army Corps of Engineers sees to it that the Mississippi's channel is dredged to maintain a depth sufficient to allow boats to pass. Markers define the edges of the safe zones for boats. From Baton Rouge to Cairo, the depth is kept at a steady twelve feet. From Cairo north to Minneapolis, though, the bottom is just nine feet below the river's surface—an indication of how little water the barges and tugboats actually need.

Barges survive today not because of their speed or flexibility; compared with trains and trucks, they have neither. But thanks to their enormous capacity, it can be a good deal cheaper to move goods by barge, especially in light of fuel costs, and river travel

A modern Mississippi River barge leaves New Orleans.

consequently remains a reasonable alternative even today. The barges of the twenty-first century may lack the romance of birchbark canoes and the early steamboats. Still, they are the right choice, economically speaking, for the Mississippi today.

3

....

Resources and Livelihoods

Over the years, the Mississippi River has played a vital role in the agricultural and industrial development of the United States. From the owners of small farms to the operators of towering power plants, the river has provided a major source of income for millions of people and contributed enormously to economic growth. Today, many Americans make their living on and around the river. Many others, in the meantime, depend on the Mississippi and its resources for their jobs, their food, and their homes.

Food

From ancient times to the present, the river has fed those who live on or near its banks. Sometimes the connection is direct: The plants and animals occurring naturally within the river have for years been extremely important in the diets of river dwellers. Sometimes, though, the connection is less clear. Throughout history, farmers and hunters have made extensive use of the river's ecosystem to provide food for themselves and their families.

The most obvious source of food in the river is fish, but of the 241 species of fish that live somewhere in the Mississippi River, many, perhaps most, are rarely if ever eaten. They are too small, too bony, too hard to catch, or simply not tasty enough to be worth the effort. And some species that do make good eating are relatively uncommon in the river. Still, that leaves plenty of fish species that are an excellent source of food, and the people who live along the river make extensive use of them.

Among the most numerous and palatable fish in the river are catfish, muskellunge, sunfish, perch, and pike. Many of these species are fairly small, weighing no more than five or six pounds, and make for a good meal or two. Others, however, grow big enough to feed an entire family for several days at a stretch. For example, some varieties of Mississippi catfish are reputed to grow to nearly two hundred pounds.

The first people to catch fish in the river were the Native Americans who lived near its banks. Few, if any, of the Indians relied on fish as the major part of their diet,

Mississippi River fishermen haul in a net filled with catfish.

but most river tribes fished at least occasionally. The methods they used varied considerably. The Iowa, for instance, generally speared large fish that swam in shallow waters near the shore. Other tribes more commonly shot fish with arrows, or caught them using hooks and lines, much as modern-day anglers do.

Some Indians also created weirs, or miniature wooden fences, which they set up in the waters where fish were numerous. These weirs were essentially fish traps. They channeled the fish into an enclosure, open at one end and closed at the other. While water flowed freely between the slats of wood, large fish would have difficulty escaping. Either they had to swim against a strong current to find their way out, or the single opening was hard to find from the inside. In either case, once trapped, the fish were easy to harvest.

From Subsistence to Sport

Through the years of European exploration and settlement, fishing was a way of life along the river. It was cheap to catch fish, and not especially labor-intensive for those who lived on the river's banks. And certainly the fish were plentiful enough: The river was rich in the microorganisms that constitute the bottom of the river's food chain. As with the Native Americans, fish was not the primary source of food for European settlers, but when crops failed or game animals became scarce, the fish in the river provided a good source of food, and the people who lived on its banks seldom starved.

Indeed, fish have frequently been the food of last resort for the poorest residents along the Mississippi. Mark Twain's novel *Huckleberry Finn*, for example, describes the journey of a poor white boy and a runaway slave down the river. Although *Huckleberry Finn* is a work of fiction, it is also an accurate depiction of life along the Mississippi. Without money and forced to move stealthily to avoid capture, the two relied heavily on the river for sustenance. The pair set out fishing lines almost every day, and as often as not were successful. As Huck reported about their daily routine along one stretch of the river, "We would take some fish off of the lines [each morning], and cook up a hot breakfast."[16]

For the most part, the European settlers and their descendants used somewhat different fishing techniques than the Indians used. The Europeans introduced fishing with nets, for example, a method evidently unknown among the natives who lived along the river. The Europeans also used fishing rods and lines more than the Indians did, while making less use of spears and arrows.

Yet the new settlers were flexible and adapted their techniques to the stretches of river they fished most often. In parts of southern Mississippi, for instance, people often used long nets divided into sections by wooden rings four

European settlers used rods and lines like those shown in this 1850 painting to catch fish along the Mississippi River.

feet in diameter. The nets were tied to a tree by means of a long rope, and weighted to ensure that they would stay in position. Every other day, the fishermen would row out to their nets and check the contents. "[They] raised the line, then the net," reported observer Harlan Hubbard, who traveled by boat down the Lower Mississippi in the 1940s. "The net was [then] rolled over inboard [the boat], a feat of balance and strength."[17]

Today, Mississippi fish continue to play an important role in feeding people, but with more food choices available and increased urbanization along the Mississippi, fishing has largely become the province of recreational anglers. Many stretches of the river are visited regularly by men, women, and children eager to catch a catfish or a walleyed pike. Still, there is a small but important commercial fishing industry on the river. Commercial anglers, many of whom hold other jobs as well, catch and sell carp, catfish, shrimp, and other species.

While overfishing and pollution have cut down on the number of fish in some stretches of the river, in others the fish populations remain strong, and Mississippi River fish today end up on tables throughout the country. A recent study of the fish in a Minnesota section of the river, for instance, captured about two hundred specimens in a single cast of a net. As one observer reported, the fish protruded from the netting "like quills from a porcupine."[18]

Other Animals

The Mississippi contains and supports many animals besides fish. These, too, have been used for centuries to supplement the diets of river dwellers. The Chitimacha, for example, a tribe that lived near the river's mouth, hunted and ate alligators and turtles; they and other Indian peoples of the region also gathered shrimp and crawfish when they were available. The Ojibwa, near the river's source, hunted ducks and geese that lived on or near the river. Later settlers and travelers likewise learned to hunt and eat these birds, reptiles, and crustaceans.

Throughout the river's length, people have also relied on local mammals for food. The river's vital and varying ecosystem attracts fur-bearing animals, both large and small. Indians and early settlers alike ate such mammals as groundhogs, black bears, and white-tailed deer. As with the fish, some of these animals have become a good deal less common near the Mississippi due to the encroachment of humans—though others, such as the deer, have not. As with fishing, the hunting of these animals has increasingly become a form of recreation rather than a necessity for most people. Nevertheless, the mammals living along the river were a major resource for generations of Americans—and, in a smaller way, continue to be one today.

Agriculture

The Mississippi's greatest value to Americans as a source of food, though, has nothing to do with its animal population. Instead, it involves the rich soil that stretches east and west from the river along most of its length. The countryside along the river is largely flat and easily plowed, and the soil itself is full of nutrients. The river, then, is key to a remarkable agricultural bounty.

That is not mere chance. The Mississippi has played a major role in creating much of this farmland. Over the years, the Mississippi has been constantly at work modifying and creating the landscape through which it flows. When the river floods, it spreads muddy water across the countryside, sometimes for dozens of miles from the riverbanks. As the water recedes or evaporates, it leaves behind nutrient-rich sediment. Through time, layer upon layer of this sediment has built up, creating one of the most fertile valleys anywhere in the world.

Native American Farming

Like fishing, agriculture along the Mississippi was first practiced by the Native Americans, who recognized the fertility of the soil and made excellent use of it. Although many Indian tribes were hunters and gatherers, most of

Wild Rice

For the most part, the plants that naturally occur in and around the Mississippi are not highly valued as food for humans. There are several kinds of berries that flourish along the riverbanks, and the Mississippi has a few other types of fruit trees as well. Similarly, edible vegetables and mushrooms can sometimes be found near the river. But most of these are far from plentiful, and the food obtained from them made up only a small proportion of river dwellers' diets.

There was, and is, one notable exception. That is a species called wild rice, which grows along the northernmost stretches of the river and several of its tributaries. The name is a bit misleading: Wild rice is actually a type of grass and not rice at all. Nevertheless, it was a staple of several northern Indian peoples. Generally it was gathered by women who traveled in canoes through the shallow backwaters of the river, where the current was weak and the plant thrived. As Carl Waldman describes the process in *Encyclopedia of Native American Tribes:*

"First, the women would bend the tops of the tall aquatic grass over the canoe's side. Then they would hit the heads with a paddle, knocking the seeds into the boat's bottom. The seeds could then be dried in the sun or by fire to open the hulls; next they were stamped on or pounded; and finally they were winnowed in a birchbark tray, in the wind, to separate the hulls from the grain. The grain was usually boiled and served with maple syrup or in a stew."

Wild rice could be labor intensive to gather and prepare, but the crop was valuable. The tribes that collected wild rice not only added to their diet, but had an important trade commodity as well.

Ojibwa Indians use a canoe to harvest wild rice at the edge of the Upper Mississippi.

those who lived along the Mississippi were farmers as well, and a few obtained the largest share of their food through farming.

To be sure, there was somewhat less farming done along the northern stretches of the river than there was on the Mississippi's lower two-thirds. The colder climate, with its long winters, made agriculture less reliable, and limited the kinds of crops that could be grown by northern tribes. As a result, many Native American farms near the northern part of the river were small, perhaps more like garden plots than actual farms, and few northern peoples relied as heavily on farming as they did on other sources of food.

Farther south, however, farming was more common—and generally more important—for the Native Americans who lived along the lower stretches of the river. For example, among the Choctaw, sums up historian Carl Waldman, "hunting, fishing, and the gathering of edible wild plants were secondary in importance to their frequent plantings and harvestings."[19] The river had created a productive and fertile plain, and the Choctaw, along with other southern tribes, made good use of it.

For Native Americans in the north and the south alike, the most important crop was corn, or maize. Rich in nutrients and relatively easy to grow, corn was also frequently used as a trade commodity. Beans and squash were also commonly cultivated along the Mississippi and its tributaries. To a considerably lesser extent, so were sunflowers, sweet potatoes, and melons. All of these plants grew well in the fertile soil near the Mississippi.

Managing the plants, however, was not necessarily easy. As one historian points out, the Native Americans of the time "lacked plows, draft animals, and fertilizers, and did not know about rotating crops."[20] Hoeing and raking had to be done by hand, usually with tools fashioned from wood or animal bones. Moreover, crops generally grew better if they were planted in the fertile bottomlands of the river. Some Indians who lived farther from the river, therefore, would travel as much as five or six miles to plant their crops. The greater yield from these lands, however, made the journey worth the time and effort.

Early European Farmers

Many of the first European settlers in the Mississippi Valley migrated from small farms farther to the east. They were gratified by crop yields much greater than what they were accustomed to in their former homes. In many areas, to be sure, clearing the land was very difficult: Often it was necessary to chop down trees and, in other places, thick prairie grasses covered the land and had to be plowed under, which required even greater effort. But there were far fewer rocks to interfere with planting in the Mississippi Valley than there were in the Northeast, and the soils along the Mississippi and its tributaries were far more fertile than the sandy soils of the Southeast.

To the settlers, then, the fertility of the Mississippi region was a godsend. "Our land is of excellent quality and very productive,"[21] wrote Rebecca Burlend, an English immigrant who with her husband started a farm near the confluence of the Mississippi and the Illinois. Besides producing bumper crops of potatoes, wheat, and corn, the Burlends kept horses, pigs, sheep, cattle, and poultry, which thrived on the grain the couple grew.

Nonfood crops did well, too, especially cotton, which was extremely well suited to the fertile, boggy soil along the southern Mississippi. Planters flocked west from Georgia and Alabama to establish cotton plantations in Mississippi, Louisiana, and Arkansas. In Issaquena County, Mississippi, cotton planter Wade Hampton praised the quality of his crop as "beyond all description."[22] Certainly, this land was far better than he had been used to farther east.

These Europeans had better tools at their disposal than the Indians had had. Their tools included plows and metal rakes and hoes; they also had draft animals, such as oxen and horses, to pull their equipment. As time went

Workers harvest cotton by hand in this 1883 painting.

on, farming technology improved, and crop yields grew accordingly. Farms grew bigger, and the wilderness between them gradually disappeared. By the middle of the nineteenth century, the Mississippi Valley was in every respect the main food producer of America.

Indeed, some argued that the prairies were so fertile that successful farmers did not truly need fine tools. "All we had to do," reported a man who grew up in Iowa, "was to tickle the new-broken prairie with a harrow and a few other things . . . and it laughed with a harvest. Never was there a scene of such redundance as was exhibited by those virgin prairies at the flush of the wheat yield."[23] While the writer admitted that the labor required to grow such a crop could be hard and intense, he nevertheless was amazed at the fruitfulness of the land.

Today, much of the Mississippi Valley still is known as America's breadbasket. Illinois and Iowa each produce far more corn and soybeans than any other state. Cotton, of course, is not a food, but it grows well enough near the

The Cotton Planters

The Mississippi Delta lies where the Mississippi and the Yazoo Rivers come together in the northwestern part of the state of Mississippi. The region, an elaborate network of rivers that branch off and rejoin in sudden and unexpected ways, is one of the most fertile sections of the floodplain. The crop most often grown in the delta, however, is inedible cotton.

Before the Civil War and to an extent afterward, the delta was a booming place. Cotton was a valuable crop, and the land of the delta was a great place to grow it. The white planters who controlled the land amassed great wealth, becoming what some called a cotton aristocracy. They entered politics, sent their sons to fine colleges, and built enormous and elaborate homes. Meanwhile the majority of the residents, the poor blacks, worked harder and harder for no more reward. Few places in the South had such a disparity between white and black, rich and poor, as prevailed in the delta.

Today, with some notable exceptions, the delta is largely an economically depressed region. In many towns, there are no jobs and few prospects. Many of those with the means to leave have done so. Many African Americans, in particular, have migrated from the delta to the South Side of Chicago and other northern cities. Those who remain are disproportionately poor and uneducated, either too young to leave home or too old to start over somewhere else.

The delta still is home to a small group of wealthy white landowners who, in the words of one southern writer, as quoted in James C. Cobb, *The Most Southern Place on Earth*, "live on the incredible fiction that they don't have poverty all around them." To this extent, conditions in the delta today are a holdover from the days of the planter aristocracy, when cotton was king, personal wealth was what mattered, and the river's soil could make a man his fortune.

Black laborers such as these shown picking cotton on the Mississippi Delta in the early 1900s worked hard for low wages.

river to make Arkansas and Mississippi among the leading producers of that crop. And Minnesota leads the nation in the production of oats. Much of the reason for this productivity continues to be the rich soil laid down by the Mississippi River.

Changes Along the River

But by the beginning of the twenty-first century, farming in the Mississippi Valley was very different from what it had been in the nineteenth century—or even in the middle of the twentieth. As farming techniques and equipment grew ever more sophisticated, farms and farmers became more efficient. The amount of food produced on a single acre of Mississippi Valley farmland today is far greater than the amount produced on a comparable acre fifty or a hundred years ago. At the same time, modern farming puts a premium on size: Small farms increasingly have trouble staying in business as the costs associated with farming, such as equipment, fertilizer, and labor, rise.

Since at least the middle of the twentieth century, the trend has been for small family farmers to sell their land to large agricultural companies, which consolidate farmland under one corporate owner. Sometimes small farmers have sold their land because they are ready to change careers or because they are offered such high prices that it would make little sense to refuse. However, more often the farmers are selling because they have to: Out of money and often out of hope, they have no real choice but to sell their farms to large "agribusinesses," or farming corporations.

This trend has been particularly pronounced in the Midwest, along the Upper Mississippi. The consolidation of farms has caused great dislocations in many communities along the upper river and its tributaries. It is hard for men and women whose families have farmed for generations to leave the land, prompting some hostility toward the giant businesses buying the land, as well as toward elected officials whose policies have negatively affected the family farmers along the river.

Indeed, despite the fertility of the soil along the Mississippi, farming is a risky business and financial ruin is always a threat. "In the early 1980s," reports an observer about one region of the upper river, "farm profits vanished, land values declined and orders for new machinery and equipment dried up. The result was a depression in western Illinois and neighboring Iowa."[24] Similar situations have played out many times along the river, notably during financial panics in the late nineteenth century, during the Great Depression of the early 1930s, and during the 1980s. Farmers and economists agree that similar problems will beset farmers in the future as well.

Business and Industry

While the Mississippi has been key to food production, it has been an important source of livelihoods in other ways, too. The ease of river transportation has helped make some cities along the river important industrial and commercial centers. Four of the country's largest metropolitan areas—New Orleans, Memphis, St. Louis, and Minneapolis-St. Paul—lie directly on the Mississippi's banks, and many smaller urban centers line the riverbanks as well. While some of these communities began life as farm markets, reliant on the valley's bounty for existence, they have since become vital business hubs in ways that go far beyond agriculture.

Minneapolis, for instance, started life as a mill town, where St. Anthony's Falls—now near the center of downtown—powered grain mills. Through its early years, Minneapolis owed its survival to the falls and the farms in the region that supplied wheat to the mills. Over time, though, the city expanded, and its economy diversified. Today, Minneapolis is home to many banks, high-tech firms, and other companies whose operations have little or nothing to do with farming.

At the other end of the river, similarly, New Orleans got its start as a commercial port. The city remains an important shipping center today—it is where cargo is usually

transferred between Upper Mississippi barges and ocean-going freighters—but it has diversified in ways the city's founders could not have imagined. Today, the river in much of Louisiana is lined with refineries for the petroleum pumped from undersea wells in the nearby Gulf of Mexico. The city also has its share of banks and other businesses unrelated to the river itself.

St. Anthony's Falls (background) allowed the city of Minneapolis to thrive first as a mill town.

Some cities along the Mississippi, in fact, have become primarily factory towns, although agriculture may remain at the heart of the local industries. Dubuque, Iowa, for instance, became an important center for meatpacking and for the manufacture of farm equipment. Other cities have expanded their shipping interests to include forms of transportation that do not necessarily use the river: St. Louis, for example, became a major hub of the railroad industry, and Memphis is home to Federal Express, which specializes in shipping small parcels by air.

Tourism

Regardless of their current economic bases, nearly all Mississippi River towns were originally built to take advantage of the river, some as centers of shipping, others as farm markets. Ironically, especially in the second half of the twentieth century, many of these towns did their best to cut themselves off from the Mississippi. "The Twin Cities [of Minneapolis and St. Paul]," wrote author Jonathan Raban in 1981, "went about their business as if the river didn't exist. No road that I could see led down to it."[25]

More recently, though, many of the towns along the river have found that their proximity to the water can boost their economies. Fish and wildlife refuges dot the river's course; so do state and local parks. An increasing

A paddlewheel steamboat, outfitted as a casino, floats on the Mississippi River.

number of communities along the river are marketing the Mississippi to tourists. A federally designated scenic highway, the Great River Road, runs along both sides of the river for most of its length. One study estimates that recreational use of the river brings more than $1 billion a year to the river communities—and creates eighteen thousand jobs.

Even riverboats are making a comeback along the Mississippi. During the 1960s and 1970s, a handful of replica steamers cruised the river, offering tourists the chance to see the Mississippi as travelers did more than a century ago. The success of those ventures expanded the business. Today, virtually every good-sized community has at least one boat used to haul passengers out onto the river for short trips, and several riverboats offer longer excursions on the Mississippi and its tributaries. Other riverboats are permanently moored in the river and offer casino gambling. All of these tourist attractions have helped to provide job opportunities and extra income to the towns and their residents.

Regardless of whether people come to the Mississippi to fish, to swim, or to gamble, tourism in general has become very big business along the river. In a sense, the river has come full circle. Once, the Mississippi was the greatest asset of the communities on its banks. Today, in another way, it can be so again.

4

. . . .

Floods

For all the beauty and benefits the Mississippi offers, it also occasionally visits havoc on those who live nearby. One of the hallmarks of the Mississippi River is its propensity to flood. The river has overflowed its banks on countless occasions. While this flooding does not usually cause massive death tolls, the damage to property is often enormous, as is the disruption to daily life. Since the very earliest European settlers arrived, people have done their best to control and channel the Mississippi, thereby eliminating the danger of flooding. But throughout history, the river has successfully resisted those efforts.

Overflow and Flood Control

As is the case with many rivers, the Mississippi does not contain the same amount of water year-round. Instead, its flow follows certain seasonal patterns. In the spring, after the snow melts along the upper part of the river, the water rises and the current gradually speeds up as more and more water joins the channel. By the middle of May, snowmelt is nearly complete, the spring rains are more or less over, and water levels in the upper part of the river are

Water Levels on the Lower River

The flow of the Lower Mississippi follows seasonal patterns that are somewhat more complicated than those on the northern stretches of the river. The lower river is partly made up of the flow from the Upper Mississippi, but it is also formed from the waters of the Ohio and the Missouri, and these rivers have a different pattern of high water than does the Mississippi as it flows down to Cairo.

Along the Missouri, for instance, harsher weather delays the snowmelt. As a result, the highest water does not arrive until the end of June; but because the rainfall tends to be less along the Missouri's route, the water level usually drops rapidly after that. On the Ohio, on the other hand, the high water comes correspondingly early—often as soon as the beginning of April.

Some years, the varying patterns of high water are complementary. Typically—and ideally, for those who live along its banks—the Lower Mississippi rises soon after the Ohio does, in mid-April. A month later, when the Upper Mississippi is at its fullest, the lower river can accommodate the extra water because the Ohio has subsided. By the time the Missouri takes its turn, similarly, the Upper Mississippi is no longer so full. Thus, in a good year, the Lower Mississippi runs at or near its peak from about the middle of April all the way through June.

But not all years are "good" years where the river's capacity is concerned. Some years two—or even three—of the main rivers approach their high-water levels at the same time. The problem is made worse when rainfall has been high near the Lower Mississippi, or when some of the river's other tributaries are fuller than normal. When that happens, the lower river gradually and inevitably rises over its banks.

at or near their peak. The lower river, farther downstream and affected by other rivers as well, rises somewhat later in the year and stays high longer.

Much of the time, the river's banks are high enough to contain even the peak water levels. But problems can arise in years when there is unusually high precipitation. A particularly heavy accumulation of snow during the course of a winter, for instance, may overload the river once it melts. Similarly, heavy rainfall in early spring can result in dangerously high water levels in the river. Under such conditions, the excess water spills over the Mississippi's banks and through the adjoining countryside.

Among the rivers of the world, the Mississippi is one of the most complicated to manage when it comes to flooding. That is true in part because it does not flood every year, unlike, say, the Nile or the Amazon, whose floods are highly predictable. Because there are years without floods, people complacently come to believe that flooding is an unusual state of affairs; thus, they build homes, farms, and businesses in areas subject to flooding.

Thus, in comparison with rivers that flood like clockwork every April or May, whose developed areas are kept at a distance, the Mississippi's banks tend to be lined with towns, farms, and buildings. The commuter airport in St. Paul, Minnesota, for instance, is built on low-lying land that has been flooded several times in the 1990s, making the airport virtually unusable for weeks or months each time.

In some river cities, neighborhoods are covered by water two years of every three. Others are saved from similar fates only by flood control devices, such as levees, which are earthen walls that serve to raise the height of the river's banks. "Something like half of New Orleans is now below sea level," writes John McPhee. "The river goes through [the city] like an elevated highway."[26]

Early Attempts

The Indians who lived along the river's edge did not attempt to control the floods at all. Instead, they sensibly kept their distance. The Native Americans "build their houses on the high land," reported an early observer; "and where there is none, they raise mounds by hand and here they take refuge from the great flood."[27]

Even if the Indians miscalculated the flood's height, however, disaster was unlikely. When the river floods, it rises slowly from one day to the next; flash floods along

the Mississippi are quite rare. Moreover, the Native Americans who lived along the Mississippi rarely built permanent structures. Thus, it was simple to move to higher ground. And while the river's overflow might destroy a year's crop, few Indian tribes relied so heavily on agriculture as to be faced with famine if a crop was lost.

It was therefore left to the Europeans, who did build permanent structures and who did depend heavily on agriculture, to try to control the river's rise. Their first attempts were levees. These were modest structures, perhaps four to six feet high at the most. In 1726, the newly established community of New Orleans constructed the first of these. Although much of the city had been built on relatively high ground, the elevation had proved insufficient to keep the waters at bay, and an engineer directed that a levee be raised along the banks of the Mississippi "more effectively to preserve the city from overflow."[28]

Few Native American tribes built permanent structures along the river and so could readily move settlements such as the one shown in this painting.

The Banks of the River

Some observers of the Mississippi argue that, in a sense, the river's banks actually spread out to the limits of its floodplain. To map the river, under this definition, would require finding the highest level of water, seeing how far in each direction it travels, and marking the boundaries of the river at that point. Obviously, much of that area is dry nearly all of the time, and it would be silly to try to canoe or fish in a spot ten miles from the river's normal course; the definition, then, does not make sense for all purposes.

Still, the notion of the river covering all that territory serves as a useful reminder of the Mississippi's tendency to flood. In this view, it is not so much that the river overflows its banks as that it reclaims its own territory. "The river's natural flow-way," writes Hodding Carter in *Lower Mississippi*, discussing the days before European settlement, "was some forty miles wide." Left to its own devices, that is, the river would claim all the land for twenty miles on each side. Anyone who tried to build permanent settlements in that area was taking a big risk.

More Levees

For all anyone knew at the time, one small levee was sufficient. But it was not. As New Orleans grew, the levee grew, too. At first it was merely lengthened. Within eight years of its beginnings, the dike stretched a distance of forty miles. The mound of earth did succeed in keeping the floodwaters away from New Orleans. However, the walls did not keep the river from swelling. And with the New Orleans side of the river confined, flooding on the opposite bank worsened considerably.

That still did not seem to be a major issue for the area's residents. The natural flow of the river had not been seriously disrupted. The walls simply prevented excess water from flowing in one direction. But when some people decided to settle on the other side of the river, the situation became more complicated. Taking a lesson from New Orleans, these settlers promptly built their own levees to keep the water out.

By 1812, less than a century after the building of the first levee, a continuous row of dikes ran along both sides of the river from New Orleans north for over a hundred miles. The levees were built strong: They did not crumble or disintegrate under the force of the current. However, with both sides of the river effectively blocked, excess water rose higher. Before long the original height of the levees was clearly inadequate to contain a rising river. Through that hundred-mile stretch, the river routinely rose over the top of the levees and flooded the towns anyway.

In response, the citizens of New Orleans and the surrounding communities simply added earth to the tops of the levees, pushing them to ten, twenty, and even forty feet above water level. As a stopgap measure, this tactic made sense: The levees, if built high enough, could in theory keep out any amount of water. But as an overall plan

In this 1863 drawing, workers repair a damaged New Orleans levee.

of flood control, levees were impractical. It was not possible to build forty-foot levees along the length of the entire river.

Nor was raising levees desirable. As author John Barry points out, high levees are extremely risky for the people who live behind them. Under ordinary circumstances, the river swelled slowly, allowing people plenty of time to escape from the floods. But the levees changed that. "If a levee towering as high as a four-story building gave way," he writes, "the river could explode upon the land with the power and suddenness of a dam bursting."[29]

Problems with the Levees

Nor, in the end, did the higher levees do all that much to contain flooding. The high waters continued to come down the Lower Mississippi, damaging areas without dikes and occasionally punching small holes in existing levees, permitting water to escape into the streets of the communities behind them. Despite the New Orleans levees, great floods were recorded along the lower river four times in the fifteen years from 1782 to 1796, and many times thereafter as well. In 1809, for instance, an observer reported "a disastrous flood, which . . . inundated all the plantations near Natchez [about two hundred miles upriver of New Orleans] and destroyed all the crops."[30]

Residents watch as floodwaters from the Mississippi destroy much of New Orleans during an 1858 flood.

In some respects, the most sensible response to the floods would have been to stop building permanent settlements on the river's edge, and to move away from the rising waters as the Indians had done. But even by the early nineteenth century, moving was not a viable option. Too many towns lay directly in the path of the floods; too much money had been invested in buildings, streets, and ports to justify letting nature take its course. Perhaps even more important than towns and structures was the farmland. "The fertile earth beside the river," writes Hodding Carter, "is a prize worth withholding from overflow."[31]

However, if moving from the river was not an option, then it was increasingly clear that the levee system needed rethinking. One obvious problem was that the levee system lacked any kind of coherence. Levees along the river varied in height and strength. Some well-funded communities built sturdy levees with public monies while others were too poor to build any levees at all. One response to this problem was to get the federal government's help in constructing and maintaining the dikes. In 1850, for example, a law gave Louisiana, Arkansas, and Mississippi thirty-two thousand square miles of national land "to construct the necessary levees and drains to reclaim the swamp and overflow lands therein."[32]

But at the same time, some observers thought that such measures were not particularly helpful. In their view, the problem was not that the levees were poorly constructed or badly maintained: The problem was that they were simply not up to the task of controlling floodwaters. These people advocated two entirely different solutions to flood control: outlets, or spillways, and cutoffs.

Outlets and Cutoffs

The idea behind outlets was simple enough. Floods, after all, were created by an excess amount of water coming down the Mississippi's main channel. If some of that water could be diverted elsewhere, then the water level in the river itself would subside. The proponents of outlets argued that channels should be created linking the lower river to lakes, ponds, and other nearby streams. The channels would not be needed during times of low water; but when flooding came, they would serve to draw off some of the torrent.

The theory behind cutoffs was also fairly simple. In this proposal, engineers planned to straighten the course of the river by artificially creating cutoffs at strategic points along its route. The thinking was that the cutoffs would speed the waters on their way. The faster the river, scientists reasoned, the less opportunity the waters would have to back up, and the less chance there would be of massive flooding.

Outlets and cutoffs both made a certain amount of intuitive sense. Despite the increasing problems with levees during the 1850s and 1860s, though, both suggestions were greeted with scorn by many of the country's most influential engineers. Sometimes these men were simply mistaken in their information or their reasoning. At other times they seemed motivated more by petty personal squabbles rather than a search for science. Whatever the reason, these engineers utterly dismissed the idea of replacing the levees with outlets or cutoffs.

In 1861, the pro-levee forces won out. Andrew Humphreys, the chief engineer of the U.S. Army, and a virulent critic of outlets and cutoffs, delivered an official report on the subject of flood control. "The plan of levees," concluded Humphreys, "may be relied upon for protecting all the alluvial bottom lands liable to inundation below Cape Girardeau [Missouri]."[33] With a few small local exceptions, the construction of levees continued to be the only method of flood control used on the river.

The Flood of 1927

The flooding persisted. A damaging flood struck Mississippi and Arkansas in 1862; many families moved several dozen miles inland to escape the rising waters. Three years later, the same region was devastated by another flood, which crumbled a mile of levee into the river and left most of the area covered by water for months. Catastrophic floods struck again along various places in the river in 1874, 1882, and 1884, and then hit during four different years in the 1890s.

Governments responded to each flood in the same way: by ordering more levees to be built, and by ordering existing levees to be strengthened and made ever higher. Each time, writes John McPhee, "pronouncements were... forthcoming that the river was at last under control and destructive floods would not occur again."[34] But each time, the officials and the scientists were proved wrong. The floods returned within just a few years.

What was worse, the level of water in the river seemed to be growing steadily higher with each new flood. The reason is clear enough today: Each new levee along the Mississippi was forcing more of the river into narrow confines, from which it had nowhere to go but up. The more levees, the higher the water level; in turn, the higher the water level, the more need there was for levees. The engineers were in a neverending and unwinnable battle against the forces of nature. Unfortunately, the men who set flood-control policy could not so easily see the consequences of their actions.

Matters came to a head along the Lower Mississippi in 1927. That year, rain began to fall early across much of the central part of the country. By early April, the water was already lapping at the top of the levee near Greenville, Mississippi. In the middle of the month, an enormous storm dropped up to fifteen inches of rain across most of the Mississippi's already sodden drainage basin. The water rose, and rose, and then rose some more, churning and roiling. Onlookers at the river had never seen it so powerful or threatening. "I saw a whole tree just disappear," recalled one man who was working on the riverbank that day, "sucked under by the current, then saw it shoot up, it must have been a hundred yards away. Looked like a missile fired by a submarine."[35]

The waters of the Mississippi River fill the streets of Greenville, Mississippi, during the 1927 flood.

A week later, the Mississippi had swollen beyond recognition. The levees could not be expected to hold so determined a current, and indeed they could not. Over the next few days, a wall of water swept down the channel, overwhelming everything in its path. By one count, the dikes failed in 227 places along the river. Some of the failures were small and easily reparable breaks, but many more represented the outright collapse of a stretch of levee. And where the levees held, they were usually too low to prevent the water from streaming over their tops.

The resulting flood was by far the worst in the river's recorded history. At its height, floodwaters covered the land surrounding the lower third of the river for twenty-five miles or more in each direction; the water actually spread almost seventy-five miles east of Greenville, Mississippi, built along the river's bank. The flooding and its aftereffects killed hundreds of people and left perhaps 1 million more homeless. Whole towns were covered up to the rooftops of the tallest houses. Others were destroyed entirely, their buildings reduced to rubble and swept downstream.

More Flooding

In the wake of the flood, Congress passed the Flood Control Act of 1928. This law did make a few important changes in flood-control policies. While unwilling to

New Orleans or the Countryside?

The flood of 1927 forced officials to make several hard choices. The most controversial involved the safety of New Orleans. As the river grew steadily higher, city leaders feared that the river would demolish the levees and damage the city beyond recovery. Their best solution, they decided, was to deliberately dynamite the levee along the eastern bank of the Mississippi near the city.

The New Orleans leaders knew that this action almost certainly would flood two nearby lightly settled parishes, or counties, to the east of their city—parishes that otherwise would have been spared the flooding. Property damage would be high, and fishermen and trappers might well lose their livelihoods. But the people could be easily evacuated, if necessary, and the action would divert enough water from the Mississippi to save the much more populous and commercially important New Orleans.

To sway public opinion outside of their city, and to earn permission from the federal government to carry out their plan, businessmen and politicians pledged to reimburse the residents of the flooded-out areas for their losses. The money would come from city coffers and from the pockets of the men and their businesses. The pledge convinced the federal government, and the men ordered the levee destroyed.

New Orleans was saved, and in fact spared any significant flooding at all. The two parishes, in turn, were inundated, and economic recovery took years. Sadly, the officials did not keep their promise. They repaid the flood victims just a few cents, if that, for every dollar of their losses, and when the case went to court, the judges ruled against the victims. It was among the ugliest moments of a very ugly flood.

remove levees altogether—indeed, the act called for strengthening and rebuilding those affected by the flood—the government authorized other methods as well, for example, the use of dredges on the lower river and dams along its tributaries, intended to increase the channel's capacity and control the amount of water entering it. For the first time, the act made use of outlets—notably a spillway leading to Lake Pontchartrain near New Orleans—and cutoffs, including one to speed the river through southern Missouri.

These measures helped ease the threat of flooding on the Mississippi, at least temporarily. In 1937, another deluge barreled down the river, but was safely diverted into Lake Pontchartrain and from there into the gulf. Still, the 1937 flood caused damage above the outlet. And it was followed by many more floods in the next several decades. There seemed to be no good answers to the problem of Mississippi flooding.

St. Charles County, Missouri, suffered $26 million in property damage due to flooding in 1993.

That point was driven home forcefully after a catastrophic flood along the upper river in the spring and summer of 1993. For weeks, the water levels rose just as they had along the lower river in 1927, and people were

powerless to stop the rise. Waters covered most of the business district of Davenport, Iowa; St. Charles County, Missouri, alone suffered $26 million in property damage.

Volunteers worked tirelessly to strengthen and raise existing levees, but much of their work was in vain. Observers counted over one thousand different breaks in the dike system. The floods forced the closing of bridges and roadways, and thousands of square miles of crops were ruined. Much of the Upper Midwest was declared a disaster area by federal authorities.

Lessons of the Flood

On the one hand, the flood of 1993 was caused by one factor, and one factor only: the weather. It was indeed a wet winter and spring across much of the Midwest, and the extra water carried by the Mississippi was a direct result of the unusually high rainfall and snowmelt within the river's drainage basin. To have stopped the flooding, given the height and force of the cresting river, would have been virtually impossible no matter what methods of flood control were used.

On the other hand, if circumstances had been different, the rain might not have been so serious a problem. Yet, there is no question that large-scale floods are growing more frequent, even during years when precipitation levels do not seem particularly high. Between 1993 and 2001, for instance, there were four one-hundred-year floods along the river—floods, that is, of such magnitude that they would ordinarily be expected to come along once every hundred years. (The 1993 flood was actually a five-hundred-year flood, but few observers expect five hundred years will pass before another one like it arrives.) To have four of these in a period of less than a decade suggests dramatically that the measures taken to control the flooding are not as successful as they might be.

One continuing problem is the levee system, still the main form of flood control along the river. While levees do help protect individual stretches of land from the river,

Without a Wall

Only one city along the Upper Mississippi lacks any kind of flood-wall to protect its downtown. That is Davenport, Iowa, which has steadfastly refused to install a wall despite several catastrophic floods over the years. The decision is highly controversial, and is constantly being reevaluated.

The issues are not easily resolved. On the one hand, Davenport has sustained a good deal of damage over the years because of its choice. The 1993 flood devastated downtown; dozens of civic and commercial buildings were badly damaged, and the city's minor league baseball team was forced to play most of its games on the road due to a flooded stadium. The lack of a floodwall results in heavy expenses for residents and taxpayers alike, detractors point out. And since recurrent flooding is likely in the foreseeable future, they add, it is fool-hardy not to take steps to protect the city.

On the other hand, those who do not want floodwalls point out that even the flood of 1993 affected only a small por-tion of the city, as much of the town is built on a hill beyond the reach of the floodwaters. Moreover, Davenport is often considered to have one of the most attractive business districts of any city along the upper river, a quality which many attribute to the absence of a wall, making the river an integral part of downtown. And a floodwall would be very costly to install and maintain, as well.

For now, Davenport continues to live without a wall, a decision that some residents applaud and others decry. The debate in many ways reflects the debates on flood-control policy in general, which remains unresolved.

Mississippi floodwaters lap at the walls of the baseball stadium in Davenport, Iowa, in 2001.

it is increasingly clear that they also result in dangerously high water levels. They have other problems as well. The higher the wall along one side of the channel, the more likely it is that flooding will occur on the other. Thus, communities scramble to make their levees taller and stronger than their neighbors' across the river, leading to what one environmentalist calls "a levee war."[36]

At their worst, these clashes can actually turn violent. The flood of 1927 saw several attempts by residents of one community to damage levees protecting another town across or farther up the river, and prompted armed patrols guarding levees from outside "invaders." Even without violence, though, the levees foster competition among the towns, in stark contrast to the cooperation that might actually help to solve the problem of flooding along the length of the river.

It is also increasingly clear that building patterns are partly to blame for the growing risk of flooding. As people expand river cities and towns, build roads, and fill in wetlands to create farmland, the soil becomes less able to absorb the rainfall. "Before [white] Americans settled the area," writes Michael Grunwald, "raindrops used to take their time getting to the river. Many pooled in swamps, bogs, and 'prairie potholes.' Others lingered in the soil. But not anymore." Since the arrival of settlers, Grunwald continues, "over half the basin's wetlands have disappeared, including more than 80 percent in Iowa, Missouri, and Illinois."[37] The effect is to move rainfall and snowmelt into the river much more quickly than ever before, filling the river during seasons of high water and increasing the risk of flooding downstream.

Changes and Strategies

The 1993 flood did lead to a few small changes in flood policy. Most notable of these was a move to limit or prevent people from rebuilding in zones prone to regular flooding. Officials in East Dubuque, Illinois, for instance, are trying to close off a low-lying neighborhood, bulldoze sixty or so houses, and return the area to wetlands. The homeowners are being offered assistance to build or buy elsewhere. And the entire town of Valmyer, Illinois, farther downstream, was moved to higher, safer ground after it was essentially demolished by the onrushing waters.

But in the end, the 1993 flood has not led to many changes in flood-control measures. The heavy reliance on levees is not likely to change soon: Too much money and effort have been invested in them, and there is no clear alternative. Outlets have been effective, but in many places along the river they are impractical for topographic reasons; cutoffs are a reasonable temporary solution, but the Mississippi has a way of finding its own course. And wetland destruction, despite a few efforts to salvage what remains, continues.

There are no easy answers to the problem of flood control. And there may be no answers at all, difficult or easy, because in the end the Mississippi is simply too powerful to be controlled. The river does what it does, regardless of the desires of human beings and the effect upon them. As Mark Twain put it: "Ten thousand river commissions, with the minds of the world at their back, cannot tame that lawless stream, cannot curb it or confine it, cannot say to it, Go here, or Go there, and make it obey; cannot save a shore which it has sentenced; cannot bar its path with an obstruction which it will not tear down, dance over, and laugh at."[38]

5

....

Ecological Damage
and Restoration

The Mississippi River may not be the most ecologically compromised of American waters, but its health is far from perfect. The quality of its water has deteriorated considerably since European settlement began. Discharges from factories, runoff from fertilizers and pesticides, and piles of ordinary trash have cluttered and contaminated the Mississippi and damaged the overall ecosystem. In many places along its course, populations of fish, plants, and animals have been reduced or stressed. These changes have had a serious impact on the Mississippi's health; they have made the river much more fragile and vulnerable to stresses.

Stresses to the Ecosystem

The stresses to the river's ecosystem come from several sources. The biggest problem is simply the human desire to build on the floodplain and as near to the river as possible. The trend along the Mississippi, as in much of the rest of the nation, is for humans to move steadily into areas that were once rural and untouched. Shopping malls, roads, and subdivisions spring up in areas that a year or two earlier were home to ducks and other wildlife. Along the Mississippi, urban spread in large cities such as St. Louis and New Orleans continues, and smaller towns from Minnesota to Louisiana are growing too.

The developments destroy the immediate surroundings, of course, but their impact goes further. On the Mississippi, of course, low-lying ground is usually wet and swampy. As artificial structures go into these areas near the river, builders often find it necessary to dry up marshy areas teeming with life. But when these areas dry, the species that lived there and relied on moisture for their survival have few choices: They must either leave or die.

While houses, stores, and public buildings are a major culprit in the loss of natural land, farms have had a generally negative impact on the Mississippi ecosystem as well. The widespread clearing of land has stressed the populations of some species: Trees are the most obviously affected but birds that nested in the trees, insects that ate the bark, and smaller plants that thrived in the bed of leaves that fell each autumn also suffer. And farmers, too, have filled in more than their share of wetlands along the river, in the hopes of producing crops on formerly swampy land. These fills affect local wildlife but also influence larger ecosystems: For example, the Mississippi is one of several major American flyways, paths followed by migratory birds. Without the wetlands to use as resting places, the birds have a more difficult time making the trip.

Stress has come, too, from human attempts to tame the river. The construction of levees prevents water from getting into people's basements and washing away their houses, but levees also keep water from replenishing the wetlands that still remain untouched. Moreover, by confining the water to narrower and deeper channels, the levees change the currents, affecting wild animals and plants. Cypress trees, for instance, need a year or two on dry land to begin their growth, but the levees can create stretches of river that never dry out.

Likewise, human attempts to improve navigation have not necessarily been good for wildlife. By holding water in place, the locks and dams along the Upper Mississippi can alter the temperature of the river, making it less hospitable to some species. Dredging channels for navigational purposes similarly stirs up sediment, which has an effect on certain plants. "Sedimentation blocks light, prohibiting photosynthesis," points out conservationist Jeff Stein. Along certain stretches of the river, the excess silt means that, in Stein's words, "you have very little opportunity for marsh plants to grow."[39]

A flock of white pelicans flies over the Mississippi Delta in search of a favorable resting place.

Extinctions and Dwindling Species

While some of these individual changes are small, the interdependence of wildlife along the Mississippi means that any environmental change can have a great impact. If marsh plants do not grow because of excessive sedimentation, then the birds that eat them lack food. If insects disappear because they are denied a wetland for breeding, then the fish that prey upon them will die. And if levees make it harder for cypress trees to grow, then the small reptiles, amphibians, and fish that hide among the roots of the trees will be eaten by predators.

As a result of these small environmental changes, the Mississippi is rapidly losing many species. The number of canvasback ducks, for instance, has dropped significantly on the upper river below Davenport, Iowa. Sturgeon populations on the lower river are diminishing rapidly, and largemouth bass are dwindling along most of the upper river. As species decline or vanish, the diversity of the ecosystem is being lost—a diversity that most biologists agree is vital to a healthy river.

To be sure, the environmental changes have been a boon to certain species, at least in the short term. The conversion of wetlands to farms, for example, is helpful to birds like starlings and sparrows that thrive in flat, dry land. Unfortunately, the species that are doing best include many that are unpleasantly aggressive or otherwise unwanted. The zebra mussel, for instance, has become common in certain stretches of the river, but it clogs intake pipes of factories and municipal water systems, fouls locks and dams, and crowds out native shellfish. It also devours small microorganisms that are food for fish. "No microorganisms, no fish,"[40] one journalist notes tersely.

Another pest is the water hyacinth, a plant that forms dense carpets of floating weeds on the river. A non-native plant, the water hyacinth has effectively displaced many native plants. By blocking sunlight and preventing easy access to the river's surface, the water hyacinth has also interfered with the survival of native fish and animals. Efforts to eliminate the water hyacinth and the zebra mussel have been unsuccessful.

The pesky zebra mussel poses a serious threat to native Mississippi fish by devouring vital microorganisms.

Pollution

Perhaps a bigger risk to the river's health, though, is pollution. Pollutants in the Mississippi impact the river as a source of water for drinking, swimming, and other uses. The pollution also has a dramatic impact on the lives of animals and plants. Moreover, polluted waters may affect wildlife and humans in ways that scientists do not yet understand. While many of the consequences of pollution are clear—drinking contaminated water can cause intestinal illness, for example, and ingesting certain river-borne chemicals can lead to cancer—some of the long-term consequences of living, working, and playing near contaminated waters remain unknown.

The pollution in the Mississippi is of three kinds. The first, and usually the most obvious to a casual observer, is trash. The current is often heavy with rusted shopping carts, broken umbrellas, beer cans, and other types of garbage. Most of this trash does not biodegrade. When it washes ashore or gets snagged in the shallows, it stays put until someone removes it.

Some of this mess is accidental, the debris swept away in floods, whose waters can carry away everything not

Water hyacinth floats inside the shell of an illegally discarded refrigerator in the Atchafalaya swamp.

fastened to the ground. Some, though, has been deliberately tossed into the river by the people who live nearby, or by those who use the Mississippi for recreational purposes. And in more than a few cases, factories have dumped trash into the river to avoid having to pay to dispose of it properly. This is less common than it used to be, but the practice continues. In one 1995 example, a Louisiana-based shipping corporation was found guilty of dumping boat engine parts, wooden pallets, and shrink wrap into the river near its headquarters.

The trash is unsightly, of course, but it has more dramatic environmental impacts as well. Nylon fishing line and shrink wrap can entangle fish and birds, ultimately killing them. Refrigerators dumped into the stream can leak chemicals into the flow of the river. Garbage piling up on a sandbar can discourage migratory birds and mammals from using the land as a place to hunt or rest. And some animals may ingest bottle caps and other small bits of refuse, choking in the process.

Industrial Discharges

Still, the effects of garbage are limited in comparison with the problems created by industrial waste. The Mississippi is lined with factories of all kinds, from small meat-packing concerns to gigantic oil refineries. Many of these plants produce waste as part of the manufacturing process, and much of that waste ends up in the river. This so-called end-of-the-pipe pollution is most common along the lower river. That is partly because waste from the

The Sewers of St. Louis

The sewage system of St. Louis high-lights some of the successes, and some of the issues, regarding pollution cleanup along the Mississippi. During the nineteenth century, St. Louis began many public works projects, including a set of pipes to carry water and sewage. The obvious place to dump the end product was into the river, so the city officials did exactly that. Virtually no one in 1850, or even 1890, concerned themselves with the possibility that the sewage would foul the river. After all, the Mississippi was large; from a strictly local perspective, the waste quickly washed downstream and away from the city.

That state of affairs lasted until 1970. That year, pressure from government, environmentalists, and the ordinary public finally got St. Louis to quite literally clean up its act. City

officials built new facilities to treat the sewage before sending it back to the river. The plants were extremely costly, but the new system's benefit to the environment was remarkable. Before the treatments began, St. Louis was dumping 300 million gallons of raw sewage every day into the Mississippi.

However, the new system is not perfect. During storms, the system cannot handle the excess water, so the facilities shut down. Then the sewage goes directly into the river, as before. The problem is the city's sewer lines, some of which are 150 years old, buried under streets and buildings, and extremely difficult to reach and replace. The price tag for replacing the outdated network would run into the billions, one official estimates. The desire to clean up the river must be balanced with the cost of doing so.

Outflow from a sewage treatment plant heads for the Mississippi near Quincy, Illinois.

Upper Mississippi washes south, and partly because antipollution laws in states such as Louisiana and Mississippi have been historically lax; but it is also because the Lower Mississippi is home to larger factories, which produce more pollution.

Similar problems exist with regard to water and sewage treatment. Many of the water and sewage facilities along the Mississippi are antiquated and inefficient; they incompletely treat the wastewater produced by river communities and dump partially purified water back into the Mississippi. Harmful as this procedure is to the river's health, it nevertheless represents an improvement over previous practices. Until the federal Clean Water Act was passed in 1972, it was common for sewage to be piped into the river raw and completely untreated.

Whether the waste comes from factories or sewage treatment plants, it remains prevalent in the river today. Currently, an estimated 300 million pounds of toxic chemicals are discharged into the Mississippi every year. Though almost every stretch of the river receives some of these pollutants, by far the largest amount—nearly one third—is discharged in the hundred-mile stretch between Baton Rouge and New Orleans. As for sewage, every day the wastewater facilities up and down the river dump a collective billion gallons of partly treated sewage into the Mississippi.

All this pollution is extremely harmful to the river's overall health. Some chemicals break down before they can do great damage, but most pollutants do not decay so quickly. Instead, they intermingle with the rest of the water, contaminating it. Sometimes the effect is obvious: Sewer discharges may float on the surface of the water, bubbling and ugly. But the pollution is usually in the form of compounds that are less visible.

There is no shortage of potentially dangerous chemicals in the Mississippi. A number of companies, for example, discharge oil and petroleum products into the river. Mercury and a family of chemicals called polychlorinated biphenyls (PCBs), along with other materials used in industrial processes, are common as well. All of these substances can kill fish and birds. They also have effects on human health; children born to mothers who ate PCB-laden fish, for instance, have had a higher than average rate of developmental disorders, and mercury has been implicated in neurological problems in humans. The pollutants are so numerous that any given stretch of river likely contains at least one toxin in concentrations unsafe for humans.

Farms and Fertilizer

The third form of pollution in the Mississippi is agricultural runoff, which largely enters the northern part of the river. Farmers often use chemicals to increase crop yields. They add chemical fertilizers to the soil, spray their fields with pesticides to reduce the damage to crops from insects, and apply herbicides to kill off weeds. The measures

DDT and the River

The most destructive pesticide in the history of the Mississippi River is a compound known as DDT. An effective killer of insects, DDT was widely used on midwestern farms during the 1950s and 1960s. Unfortunately, DDT proved to be extremely dangerous to the health and ecology of the river. It was eventually pulled from the market; but not until it had devastated the Mississippi's ecosystem.

Insects sprayed with DDT were eaten by birds and fish, which absorbed the DDT into their own bodies. The birds and fish, in turn, were devoured by larger animals, who thereby became DDT-tainted as well. The chemical built up in the tissues of the victims; it could not be excreted or sweated away like many other substances. The higher on the food chain an animal was, the more the DDT levels increased in its body.

While the pesticide affected many different animals, perhaps the most seriously impacted was the eagle. Near or at the top of the food chain, river eagles ingested astonishing amounts of DDT over a period of months or years. The chemical did not necessarily kill the birds directly, but caused the birds' eggs to have thin, easily breakable shells. The result was that eaglets hatched too early, or were crushed by the weight of their mothers' bodies. The population of eagles declined precipitously all along the river.

DDT is gone now, but its influence remains. To this day, some Mississippi catfish and birds of prey show traces of DDT in their systems. And while no current pesticide appears as damaging as those of the 1960s, scientists and conservationists are uncomfortably aware that pesticides, under the best of circumstances, are built to be toxic. They were not made to wash routinely into a body of water used by millions for drinking, swimming, and fishing; and so no one can say for sure what the long-term effects of the poisons will be on the river.

Crop dusters apply DDT to a farmer's field in this 1945 photo.

are effective. The fertilizers and other chemicals are among the reasons why the Upper Midwest produces so much food.

But the higher yields come at a price. Pesticides, for example, are washed by the rains off farm fields, into streams, and eventually into the Mississippi. These chemicals are often nearly as toxic to fish and birds that live in and around the Mississippi as they are to insects. Concentrations of the chemicals can build up to alarmingly high levels in the water. Even after the flood of 1993, which most scientists expected would dilute the pesticides and lower their effect on the river, levels of pesticides such as atrazine and metolachlor remained dangerously high.

Fertilizers, too, are washed into the Mississippi, with equally damaging consequences. Besides sometimes containing dangerous chemicals themselves, these fertilizers support the growth of aquatic plants such as algae. The extra plants consume oxygen needed by fish and other marine life. In fact, the widespread use of fertilizers creates environmental issues well into the Gulf of Mexico, where a so-called dead zone the size of Massachusetts lies directly south of the Mississippi's mouth. Virtually no sea creatures can live in the dead zone, created by excess growth of algae and a consequent lack of dissolved oxygen, or hypoxia. "You can swim and swim and not see any fish," reports a scientist. "Anything that can't move out eventually dies."[41]

Cleanup Efforts

The news on the river's health, however, is not all bad. In some ways, the river is a good deal cleaner than it used to be. Much progress has been made in purifying the river and protecting it from some of the worst pollution. The banning of the use of certain especially toxic pesticides is one example. Another is the gradual abandonment to the river of neighborhoods or entire settlements on the Mississippi's banks, allowing the floods to re-create wetlands.

Grassroots conservationist Chad Pregracke sits atop a mound of refuse retrieved from the Mississippi in 2000.

Another important change involves local cleanup efforts. Since the mid-1990s, for example, Chad Pregracke of East Moline, Illinois, has traveled the Upper Mississippi, organizing ordinary people to help pick up trash from the river. Pregracke and his crews have picked up thousands of tons of refuse, ranging from pop bottles and television sets to refrigerators and pickup trucks. "This is a good reminder that one person really can make a difference,"[42] says one of Pregracke's volunteers. Such grassroots cleanup efforts are on the upswing throughout the Mississippi Valley.

Sewage treatment plants are generally less damaging to the environment than they were in the past. The sewer systems in Minneapolis and St. Paul once pumped so much waste into the river that few fish could survive. One

The Dead Zone

The size of the Gulf of Mexico's "dead zone" varies from year to year. Depending on the height of the river, the prevalence of drought in its watershed, and other factors, the zone may be as small as seventeen hundred square miles or as large as eight thousand, although the latter figure is more common. The zone was first identified more than two decades ago, but the problem has only recently gained widespread public attention.

In 1998, President Bill Clinton appointed a committee, called the Mississippi/Gulf of Mexico Watershed Nutrient Task Force, to study the issue and to make recommendations for government action. The task force has made several suggestions to alleviate the problem. One is simply to encourage the states along the river to do a better job of monitoring the levels of nitrogen in the stream—and the levels put onto fields by farmers eager to improve their crop yields. Monitoring to date has been haphazard, with some states doing a thorough job of it and others barely doing it at all.

Another recommendation involves returning as much acreage as possible to wetlands, both to reduce the amount of fertilizer and to provide an intermediate place for excess nutrients to drain. The measure would also improve the health of the river's ecosystem in other ways. And a third suggestion is to encourage farmers to reduce the amount of fertilizer they use. While some of these programs would be voluntary, there also may be federal money available to help implement some of the measures.

To date, however, the recommendations have not been put into force. While the Clinton administration tended to be zealous in attacking Mississippi pollution issues, Congress and Clinton's successor, President George W. Bush, have been more cautious and less willing to act quickly. There are also geographic issues involved. The states of the Upper Midwest, where most of the problem originates, are far removed from the gulf, where the problem has its greatest impact. As a government official puts it, quoted by Mark Schleifstein in his article "Gulf's Dead Zone Has Gone Godzilla, Expert Says," "It's always been a challenge to get people to accept that their agricultural practices in Wisconsin or Illinois result in these problems in the Gulf of Mexico."

study found just seven species of fish in one nearby stretch of the river: "Bacteria," an observer reported, "was robbing the river of oxygen as it broke down raw and partially treated sewage."[43] In recent decades, though, the Twin Cities have cleaned up most of their sewage before dumping it. Today, the river near the cities is much cleaner, and the fish are abundant again.

Some companies, too, have voluntarily lowered the amount of pollution they pour into the Mississippi. Among the major companies which have begun releasing fewer contaminants since the early 1990s are 3M, Monsanto, and Dow, all major polluters at one time. Improved technology has made it easier to clean up the most toxic chemicals, or to avoid their use altogether. But some of these corporations have also found that it is good business—and good public relations—to treat the river as gently as possible. "It's important to our employees and the communities where we do business,"[44] points out a representative of one large company.

Lawsuits

Unfortunately, not every corporation has voluntarily cut down on the pollutants it discharges into the river. For these, pressure in the form of a lawsuit or a fine has sometimes proved necessary. While no state or federal law forbids pollution altogether, there are many laws on the books which limit the discharge of pollutants. The most notable of these is the Clean Water Act, but there are many others as well.

In theory, these laws provide a mechanism to attack companies that routinely foul the Mississippi as well as other bodies of water throughout the United States. In practice, though, they often have failed in this task. There are too many factories, and too few inspectors to monitor them. As a result, companies have been able to cut corners virtually at will. "No operator down here follows these laws,"[45] admitted a lawyer for a Louisiana company accused of breaking federal antipollution regulations.

How effective the laws can be often depends on how aggressive enforcement efforts are. Under President Bill Clinton, for example, the government became noticeably more active in going after polluters on the river. Regulators became more creative, too. In one 1995 case, the Justice Department successfully argued that one Louisiana company should be fined $250,000 for dumping pollutants into the Mississippi, and levied heavy penalties against the individual company officials who ordered the action. Government lawyers, when they brought the case to court, argued successfully that laws against ocean dumping applied in this case as well.

In a similar case from 1998, the government fined the Shell Oil Company $1.5 million for pollution released by one of its Missouri plants. The sum was high, but it was dwarfed by the rest of the penalty: Shell was also told to pay another $10 million to fund various environmental projects. Such punishments help the environment twice: once by making polluting fiscally painful, and again by providing funds to environmental initiatives.

"Part of Our National Heritage"

Regardless of the zeal with which the federal government pursues polluters, the task of conserving or restoring the damaged ecosystem of the Mississippi is too complex and difficult to be solved by any act of government alone. The shopping malls, housing developments, and schools newly built in the river's bottomlands are not going to be removed any time in the near future. Threatened or endangered species do not generally make quick comebacks, and lost habitat is slow to regenerate. Upper Mississippi farmers are unlikely to stop using chemicals on their crops altogether; and it would be impossible to eliminate all discharges of pollutants from factories and sewage treatment plants overnight.

Still, there is hope for the river. Antipollution efforts are growing, and the public seems to be increasingly vigilant. No longer can corporations expect river dwellers to ignore factories that pollute the river; no longer can municipalities blithely pour millions of gallons of sewage into the current without there being an outcry among citizens.

Some progress has been made on even the most complicated problems. For years, few people paid much attention to the rapid loss of wetlands in the Mississippi basin. Today, the loss continues, but awareness of the problem is far greater. This greater awareness has made possible passage of a few measures designed to preserve and expand important habitat. And teams of researchers are hard at work developing possible solutions to the problems of agricultural runoff in the Midwest. There are no clear solutions to these problems, but at least there is increasing acknowledgment that the issues exist.

The Mississippi River near Hannibal, Missouri. Antipollution efforts are helping the river recover its natural beauty.

In the end, most observers agree that the river is too valuable a treasure to waste. Its ecosystem has an importance that goes far beyond the river's banks, and the overall health of the Mississippi affects the health of millions of Americans. Indeed, for better or worse, the river's role in human life will continue long after the present. As then U.S. Attorney General Janet Reno put it in 1998, "The Mississippi River is part of our national heritage. We have a responsibility to restore and protect it not just for this generation, but also for all of those to come."[46]

Notes

Introduction: Two Rivers

1. John M. Barry, *Rising Tide*. New York: Touchstone, 1997, p. 38.
2. Willard Price, *The Amazing Mississippi*. New York: John Day, 1963, p. 113.

Chapter 1: The Big Muddy

3. John McPhee, *The Control of Nature*. New York: Farrar, Straus and Giroux, 1989, p. 5.
4. Mark Twain, *Life on the Mississippi*. 1883. Reprint, New York: Harper and Brothers, 1929, p. 4.
5. Quoted in Twain, *Life on the Mississippi*, p. 2.
6. Twain, *Life on the Mississippi*, p. 213.
7. Hodding Carter, *Lower Mississippi*. New York: Farrar and Rinehart, 1942, p. 3.

Chapter 2: The River as Highway

8. Quoted in Barry, *Rising Tide*, p. 38.
9. Jonathan Raban, *Old Glory*. New York: Vintage, 1981, pp. 64–65.
10. Reader's Digest, *Mysteries of the Ancient Americas*. Pleasantville, NY: Reader's Digest, 1986, p. 180.
11. Norbury L. Wayman, *Life on the River*. New York: Crown, 1971, p. 140.
12. Quoted in Carter, *Lower Mississippi*, p. 21.
13. Wayman, *Life on the River*, p. 141.
14. Ron Larson, *Upper Mississippi River History*. Winona, MN: Steamboat, 1994, p. 3.
15. Herbert Quick and Edward Quick, *Mississippi Steamboatin'*. New York: Henry Holt, 1926, pp. 130–31.

Chapter 3: Resources and Livelihoods

16. Mark Twain, *The Adventures of Huckleberry Finn.* 1885. Reprint, New York: Modern Library, 1993, p. 177.
17. Harlan Hubbard, *Shantyboat.* Lexington: University Press of Kentucky, 1953, p. 302.
18. Quoted in Greg Breining, "Urban Renewal," *Sierra*, July 1994, pp. 38+.
19. Carl Waldman, *Encyclopedia of Native American Tribes.* New York: Facts On File, 1988, p. 61.
20. Robert H. Lowie, *Indians of the Plains.* Garden City, NY: Natural History, 1954, p. 22.
21. Quoted in David B. Greenberg, ed., *Land That Our Fathers Plowed.* Norman: University of Oklahoma Press, 1969, p. 83.
22. Quoted in James C. Cobb, *The Most Southern Place on Earth.* New York: Oxford University Press, 1992, p. 14.
23. Quoted in Greenberg, *Land That Our Fathers Plowed*, p. 116.
24. Michael Barone and Grant Ujifusa, *The Almanac of American Politics 2000.* Washington, DC: National Journal, 1999, pp. 575–76.
25. Raban, *Old Glory*, p. 31.

Chapter 4: Floods

26. McPhee, *The Control of Nature*, pp. 59–61.
27. Quoted in Stanley A. Chagnon, ed., *The Great Flood of 1993.* Boulder, CO: Westview, 1996, p. 220.
28. Quoted in Carter, *Lower Mississippi*, p. 350.
29. Barry, *Rising Tide*, p. 40.
30. Quoted in Lamar T. Beman, ed., *The Reference Shelf: Flood Control.* New York: H.W. Wilson, 1928, p. 48.
31. Carter, *Lower Mississippi*, p. 350.
32. Beman, *The Reference Shelf*, p. 18.
33. Quoted in Barry, *Rising Tide*, pp. 53–54.
34. McPhee, *The Control of Nature*, p. 42.
35. Quoted in Barry, *Rising Tide*, p. 16.
36. Quoted in William Allen, "New Levees Boost Flooding Risk, Some Say," *St. Louis Post-Dispatch*, April 12, 2001, pp. C1+.
37. Michael Grunwald, "Disasters All, but Not as Natural as You

Think," *Washington Post*, May 6, 2001, pp. B1+.

38. Quoted in Chagnon, *The Great Flood of 1993*, p. 298.

Chapter 5: Ecological Damage and Restoration

39. Quoted in Associated Press, "Migratory Bird Habitat on Mississippi River Threatened, Group Says," *St. Louis Post-Dispatch*, August 27, 2000, pp. A4+.

40. Tim Renken, "Zebra Mussels Are Becoming Nuisance of the Waterways," *St. Louis Post-Dispatch*, March 4, 2000, pp. 19+.

41. Quoted in Carol Kaesuk Yoon, "Scientists Seek to Resurrect Vast Marine 'Dead Zone,'" *Denver Post*, January 20, 1998, pp. A1+.

42. Quoted in Stephanie Simon, "Wresting Refuse from the Mississippi," *Los Angeles Times*, October 15, 2001, pp. A14+.

43. Breining, "Urban Renewal," pp. 38+.

44. Quoted in Associated Press, "Migratory Bird Habitat on Mississippi River Threatened," pp. A4+.

45. Quoted in Gary Lee, "Louisiana Company's Officers Admit Fouling the Mississippi," *Washington Post*, January 6, 1995, pp. A2+.

46. Quoted in Kate Harrigan, "Feds Move to Protect Mississippi," *Pollution Engineering*, November 1998, p. 11.

For Further Reading

Ruth Crisman, *The Mississippi*. New York: Franklin Watts, 1984. A short description of the river, its characteristics, and some of its problems.

Daniel E. Harmon, *Jolliet and Marquette: Explorers of the Mississippi River*. Philadelphia: Chelsea House, 2001. Informative account of two early French explorers and their experiences on the Mississippi.

Ann Heinrichs, *La Salle: La Salle and the Mississippi River*. Minneapolis: Compass Point, 2002. A biography of La Salle and his exploration of the river.

Bruce Hiscock, *The Big Rivers: the Missouri, the Mississippi, and the Ohio*. New York: Atheneum Books for Young Readers, 1997. Descriptions of these major rivers with special focus on the events that led to the 1993 floods.

Patricia Lauber, *Flood: Wrestling with the Mississippi*. Washington, DC: National Geographic Society, 1996. A study of the 1993 flood along the Upper Mississippi, with more general information about the river and flooding as well.

Michael Pollard, *The Mississippi*. New York: Benchmark, 1998. A description of the river, with emphasis on its physical and geographic characteristics.

Works Consulted

Books

Michael Barone and Grant Ujifusa, *The Almanac of American Politics 2000*. Washington, DC: National Journal, 1999. Demographic, political, and historical data about each American state and congressional district. Includes valuable information about river areas and the political and environmental controversies that continue today.

John M. Barry, *Rising Tide*. New York: Touchstone, 1997. A compelling account of the 1927 flood along the Lower Mississippi. The book covers the political, social, and economic effects of the flood and sketches the history of flood control measures along the river.

Lamar T. Beman, ed., *The Reference Shelf: Flood Control*. New York: H.W. Wilson, 1928. A slender book dealing with issues of flood control along the Mississippi; written in the aftermath of the great flood of 1927.

Hodding Carter, *Lower Mississippi*. New York: Farrar and Rinehart, 1942. A classic of the time and still very readable today; a history of the southern half of the Mississippi, with a great deal of vivid description.

Stanley A. Chagnon, ed., *The Great Flood of 1993*. Boulder, CO: Westview, 1996. Readings, information, and photographs about the Upper Mississippi flood of 1993. Often academic in tone.

James C. Cobb, *The Most Southern Place on Earth*. New York: Oxford University Press, 1992. The history of the Mississippi Delta; thorough and well written.

Tom Downs and John T. Edge, *New Orleans*. Melbourne, Australia: Lonely Planet, 2000. A well-written and informative guidebook to the city; gives useful information about the Mississippi River and the city's connection to it over time.

David B. Greenberg, ed., *Land That Our Fathers Plowed*. Norman: University of Oklahoma Press, 1969. An anthology of letters, journals, and published accounts written by pioneers. Describes the growth of agriculture in the Mississippi Valley.

Harlan Hubbard, *Shantyboat*. Lexington: University Press of Kentucky, 1953. Hubbard and his wife lived for seven years on a homemade houseboat, which they took down the Ohio and Lower Mississippi Rivers. One of the best accounts of travel down the river system.

Ron Larson, *Upper Mississippi River History*. Winona, MN: Steamboat, 1994. Awkwardly written and hard to follow in places, but an informative look at the upper river, with special emphasis on steamboats. Larson worked on the river as a boat captain.

Robert H. Lowie, *Indians of the Plains*. Garden City, NY: Natural History, 1954. Informative book about the Plains Indians, including a few groups who lived near the Mississippi on a part- or full-time basis.

John McPhee, *The Control of Nature*. New York: Farrar, Straus and Giroux, 1989. A discussion of ways in which humans have tried to control nature for their own ends. Includes a section on the flooding of the Mississippi River, with particular regard to the river's relationship with the Atchafalaya.

Willard Price, *The Amazing Mississippi*. New York: John Day, 1963. Price traveled from Lake Itasca to Louisiana on and near the Mississippi. An accessible account of a river journey.

Herbert Quick and Edward Quick, *Mississippi Steamboatin'*. New York: Henry Holt, 1926. A history of the river, with special focus on the era of the steamboats.

Jonathan Raban, *Old Glory*. New York: Vintage, 1981. Raban, a British citizen, took a motorboat trip down the river and recorded his observations about the people and the places he encountered along the way. Raban can be extremely snide in places, but his writing is vivid.

Reader's Digest, *Mysteries of the Ancient Americas*. Pleasantville, NY: Reader's Digest, 1986. Includes information about the Mississippian culture.

Mark Twain, *The Adventures of Huckleberry Finn*. 1885.

Reprint, New York: Modern Library, 1993. The classic American novel, describing a journey by raft down much of the Mississippi by a white boy and a runaway slave.

———, *Life on the Mississippi*. 1883. Reprint, New York: Harper and Brothers, 1929. Twain was born in a river town and traveled the river several times in his life. This book includes a description of the river and the people who made their living from it.

Carl Waldman, *Encyclopedia of Native American Tribes*. New York: Facts On File, 1988. An interesting volume, with tribes listed alphabetically. Includes information on the Ojibwa, the Chickasaw, and many other groups who lived along the Mississippi.

Norbury L. Wayman, *Life on the River*. New York: Crown, 1971. Well illustrated with black-and-white photos, maps, and drawings. Focuses on the cities of the Mississippi and its tributaries; also has information about boats and river travel.

Periodicals

William Allen, "New Levees Boost Flooding Risk, Some Say," *St. Louis Post-Dispatch*, April 12, 2001.

Associated Press, "Migratory Bird Habitat on Mississippi River Threatened, Group Says," *St. Louis Post-Dispatch*, August 27, 2000.

———, "Mississippi River Ecosystem Reported in Increasing Peril," *Boston Globe*, March 8, 1994.

Greg Breining, "Urban Renewal," *Sierra*, July 1994.

Michael Grunwald, "Disasters All, but Not as Natural as You Think," *Washington Post*, May 6, 2001.

Paul Hampel, "Reno Announces Fines for Wood River Plant," *St. Louis Post-Dispatch*, September 10, 1998.

Kate Harrigan, "Feds Move to Protect Mississippi," *Pollution Engineering*, November 1998.

Terry Hillig, "Illinois Leaders Want to Stop Levee Project," *St. Louis Post-Dispatch*, December 29, 1999.

Maura Kelly, "At Home in a Midwest Flood Zone," *Boston Globe*, June 3, 2001.

Gary Lee, "Louisiana Company's Officers Admit Fouling the Mississippi," *Washington Post*, January 6, 1995.

Tim Renken, "Zebra Mussels Are Becoming Nuisance of the Waterways," *St. Louis Post-Dispatch*, March 4, 2000.

Mark Schleifstein, "Eye on Gulf Dead Zones," *New Orleans Times-Picayune*, April 13, 1998.

———, "Gulf's Dead Zone Has Gone Godzilla, Expert Says," *New Orleans Times-Picayune*, July 27, 2001.

Stephanie Simon, "Wresting Refuse from the Mississippi," *Los Angeles Times*, October 15, 2001.

Carol Kaesuk Yoon, "Scientists Seek to Resurrect Vast Marine 'Dead Zone,'" *Denver Post*, January 20, 1998.

Index

Picture Credits

About the Author

Stephen Currie is the author of many books and magazine articles, and has written extensively for Lucent Books. As a child, he attended many family picnics on the banks of the Mississippi River—mainly at Goose Island and Pettibone Park in LaCrosse, Wisconsin. In warm weather, he can be found kayaking on the Hudson River near his home in upstate New York.